645-7386

The Book of
Drinking

Triune Books

The Book of Drinking

John Doxat

Acknowledgements

J. Allan Cash 12t, b, 29t, 31tr, 39, 40tl, tr, 55, 57t, 60tl, 65, 70tl, 71t, 82tr, 84bl, br, 85tl, bl, br, 86tr, 87, 93r, 127b; Allied Breweries 40bl, 61t, b, 81t, b, 82tl, 83t, br, 95tr; Barnaby's Picture Library 40br, 45r, 46b, 47br, 48, 52b, 53b, t, 54t, 60tr, 64t, 66tl, 67b, 68tr, tl, bl, 70tr, 75, 80, 90, 114, 115b, 131tl, tr, 144; Bass Charrington Vintners 50t, 51, 82b; Booth's Distilleries 22r, 23t; Bulmer & Co. 91, 92tr, 93l; Geremy Butler 18, 24, 64b, 69b, 100, 101, 102, 103, 104, 106, 107; Stefan Buzas 29b, 92b, 116; Camera Press 57b; Christie's, London 36ll, r; Citrus Products Export Board 111; H. R. Clayton 30; Coca-Cola Export Co. 112, 113; Cooper-Bridgeman Library 125t, 134b; John Doxat 10, 23b; Editions Graphiques Ltd. 102, 107; Mark Edwards 123, 124b, 126; Mary Evans Picture Library 9, 27, 34, 35, 37, 38l, 44t, 54l, 59r, l, 67t, 70b, 71b, 76, 77, 79t, 86br, 89t, 92tl, 99, 108, 109, 110, 118, 122tl, 125br, 127t, 129, 130bl, 131br, 132t, 133, 134t; R. B. Fleming 88t; Paul Forester 13, 42tb, 43tb; French Tourist Office 38r, 49; Guinness and Son Ltd. 83bl; S. F. and O. Hallgarten 47t, bl; John Hillelson Agency 136–7; Michael Holford 2, 32, 52t; J. Howitt & Son 50b; Irish Distillers Ltd. 14, 16; Anthony James 11t, b, 13; Marshall Cavendish 120, 121; Martell and Co. 31tl, b; Novosti Press Agency 41; Picturepoint 17, 56t, b, 60, 84t, 125bl; Radio Times Hulton Picture Library 19, 79b, 88b, 105, 130tl, tr, 131bl, 132b; Scotch Whisky Association 20, 21; Sherry House 94t, b; Spectrum 28, 54b, 68br, 85tr, 86r, 114t, 115t, 119, 124t, 135, 117; Swiss National Tourist Office 62, 63, 66tr, b; Tate Gallery 122tr; Eileen Tweedy 69, 88–9, 128t; Victoria and Albert Museum 122b, 130br; Wine Institute, San Francisco 3, 44b, 38, 39t; Adam Woolfitt/Susan Griggs 95l, br, 96t, 97; Ian Yeomans/ Susan Griggs 128b.

ISBN 0 85674 017 9
Published by
Triune Books, London, England
© Trewin Copplestone Publishing Ltd 1973
Printed in Italy by
Istituto Italiano d'Arti Grafiche
Bergamo
Mohn Gordon Ltd, London

Contents

Introduction

The subject of this volume is basically so immense that it befits the author to declare its intentions – and its limitations. When one considers that complete volumes have been dedicated to one vineyard alone; that there are at least a dozen books in currency dealing just with Scotch whisky, and that merely to list wine books in print would require scores of pages, it becomes clear that there can never be the definitive single book on drinks and their production and use. So why add to this vast literature about drinking? Because, for all I have said, there is a paucity of publications that deal with social drinking in its broadest sense, written with simplicity, and designed for the reader who is not concerned with rare vintages and exotic concoctions. And, surely, the word 'drink' should not be confined too narrowly to an alcoholic connotation? A Moslem sipping his coffee is as much drinking as a Manhattan businessman downing a Dry Martini. Albeit, intelligent use of alcohol will dominate these pages, for the obvious reason that that is what most readers will expect from it.

We may readily surmise that in the dawn of mankind's history, primitive sub-humans discovered fruit and other vegetable matter fermenting in some natural vessel – a hollow tree stump or rock basin. From thirst or curiosity they would have sampled this, and found the effect pleasing. In time, with the advent of husbandry, crude alcoholic beverages would have been manufactured. When the grape was first cultivated we can only surmise; when grain was expressly fermented for beer may be vaguely dated to thousands of years BC.

What is this thing alcohol? I will indulge in no blinding-with-science: alcohol is created by the action of yeast on sugar, ie fermentation. This sugar may already be present, as in grapes or apples; or it may be produced by the malting of grain (we shall come across this when dealing with whisky). The yeast may be in the skin of grapes and apples, may be the wild yeasts abounding in the air, or may be cultivated like bakers' or brewers' yeast. The primary reaction of yeast and sugar produces basic wine or beer. To turn these into what we term spirit, distillation is required.

Knowledge of distillation is much more recent than that of fermentation. In the Far East, distillation, presumably from fermented rice, was practised perhaps 3,000 years ago. The Arabs certainly knew of it long before the secret reached Europe, though they were probably more concerned with perfumes than intoxicants. However, they gave alcohol its name, which derives from their *Al-koh'l* (kohl), the very fine powder used cosmetically, which was subsequently applied to 'refinement' of an article. To distil is to refine. Distillation has been practised in Britain for only about 1,000 years, commercially for a much shorter period.

Fine distillation was not possible until it was realised that alcohol and water vaporise at different temperatures: 78·3°C for alcohol against 100°C for water. So if an alcoholic liquor is heated to above 78° but below 100°, the alcohol (spirit) can be drawn off and the water will be left behind. This will be dealt with in a little more detail in the Spirits chapter.

Wines, beers and spirits have long played an important role in the social life of virtually all communities, civilised and primitive. They have been used medicinally, they have been abused, they have been used religiously, they have been banned legislatively and ritually (as have tea and coffee by some sects).

Alcohol, popularly called a stimulant, is actually a depressant! But, don't worry: that's why you feel better for it. By depressing centres of anxiety it relieves tensions. It lowers bodily temperature, but by dilating the arteries eases the flow of blood: Scotch is sometimes medically recommended for certain heart conditions. In moderation, for most people it stimulates the appetite, but in excess dulls it. It can be addictive, but one of the greatest medical authorities on the subject says alcohol in itself never induced illness in a truly healthy person. In fact, he praises its virtues. There is a disease – now rightly treated as such – called alcoholism. An alcoholic may be a heavy drinker, yet is not necessarily one. To an alcoholic, alcohol is a form of poison – either physically or psychologically, or both. Thanks to a sensible modern approach, alcoholism can be treated – on the premise that the patient genuinely wants to be cured. Total abstension is the only method: the patient is then still, clinically, an alcoholic but is a non-drinking one. But do not automatically confuse a heavy drinker with an alcoholic. The sources of alcoholism are various, though in every case allied to a physical or psychological weakness. The causes may be availability of cheap alcohol, a metabolic change inducing an allergy to alcohol, environment, heredity, or prohibition (or near-prohibition).

Temperance is an admirable creed. However, when it is imposed on unwilling persons by force of law it invariably aggravates the ills it seeks to obviate – and we need look no further than the still visible effects of Prohibition in the USA to see the ghastly results; also, if less immoderately, this is witnessed in countries currently having exceptionally repressive legislation on the sale of alcohol. Normally, permissive laws make for moderate drinking; a notable exception being France. In Britain, the problem of alcoholism is not acute, though it is present. In the USA alcohol may, in fact, be of current benefit: in some areas adolescents are turning to this traditional narcotic rather than to infinitely more harmful hard drugs. It may also be stated that alcohol will continue to play its part in the life of nations as long as there are humans to make and imbibe it. So let us enjoy it, with sufficient knowledge and with good sense. And it is good sense that will be my guiding rule in the ensuing work.

Liquor or spirits

In my general introduction, I mentioned briefly the origin of spirits. Probably the most universal of these is whisky (or whiskey). Whisk(e)y of a sort is made in virtually every country: there is a sort of millet-based whiskey in China. The principal whiskies are:

Scotch whisky

Scotch whisky's origins lie in the remote history of northern Britain when Irish monks, following in the wake of colonists from Ulster, brought to Scotland Christianity, the bagpipes, and, later, the primitive art of distilling. All distilled liquors have a monkish origin, for in the monasteries lay the seeds of medicine – part alchemy, part faith, part burgeoning science – and early distillations were for medicinal rather than social purposes. All distillations have a common denominator in *aqua vitae* (water of life), in itself carrying a half-mystical, half medical connotation. The Gaelic *usquebeathe (usquebae etc.)* – whence derives the word whisky – is a version of aqua vitae.

The earliest evidence of whisky as a serious product was a mention in 1494. It was known at the royal court of Edinburgh at that time and in 1505 production was placed under the jurisdiction of the Royal College of Surgeons, the first of a series of efforts to regulate whisky. Not until 1644 was an endeavour made to tax the spirit – at sixpence a gallon.

It is sometimes surmised that the Scottish climate aided the development of whisky, since much grain must have become damp and consequently commenced to sprout fortuitously. Not to waste the grain, an obvious use for it would have been to malt it, a process manifestly known at least by the 15th century in Scotland. Malting is the first step in making whisky. Certainly it has been climate which, in differing ways, has played a vital role in the success of Scotch whisky.

Whisky distilling was originally a cottage industry. Most crofters became distillers, perhaps just for their family, perhaps for a narrow locality. Nor were the cities without alcoholic stimulants. In 1777 (to skip ahead) there existed in Edinburgh six registered stills and an estimated 300 illicit ones. The year 1707, which saw the governmental union of Scotland and England, brought into existence a Board of Excise which was notably unsuccessful in taxing whisky. After the final rebellion by the Scots in the tragic uprising of 1745, the excisemen – gaugers, as they are still called – penetrated the fastnesses of the Highlands, but vain were there endeavours to regulate the production of whisky. In 1823 alone they uncovered 13,000 illegal stills – but that apparent success no more than touched the periphery of uncontrolled distilling, so universal was it.

Thanks to some great Scottish landowners, who wielded more influence than distant Westminster, workable regulations were introduced and enforced in 1824 and thereafter the production of whisky in Scotland showed signs of becoming an industry. This roughly coincided with the invention of the Coffey (or patent) still, which allowed continuous distillation as opposed to the individual distillations of the traditional pot-still. The Coffey stills made, from a wash of mainly unmalted grain, a lighter flavoured whisky than came from the pot-stills. This eventually led to a great battle between malt and grain whiskies, manufacturers of the latter claiming sole right to the description whisky. This was resolved, and today's mighty Scotch whisky industry is a happy amalgam of malt and grain. Almost no straight grain whisky is sold for general consumption (the only one I know of is Old Cameron Brig), and, though straight malt enjoys increasing popularity, it represents only a tiny proportion of the Scotch consumed by the public the world over. Blends totally dominate the market.

Blending was invented in the 1860s. It combined the pungency of the pot-distilled malt whiskies – essentially (but not entirely) associated with the highlands – with the lightness of the grain whiskies produced by continuous distillation, a rather technical process. Until blending came in, Scotch whiskies were little relished outside their native land, though Queen Victoria and Sir Walter Scott had done much to popularise things Scottish. A few canny Scots thought that these new blended whiskies might be more to the taste of the effete southerners than the robust straight malts. They were entirely correct. They had an ally in due course in the phylloxera scourge which, in decimating French vineyards, caused a dearth of French Cognac, traditional spirit of the upper-class Englishman. But it was not only luck. Men of the calibre of James Buchanan and the Dewar brothers were tremendous salesmen and pioneers of beverage advertising: they were to succeed beyond even their wildest dreams when they took the road to London in the 1880s. Though a product of Scotland, arguably it was from London that Scotch whisky started its commercial march to global supremacy.

'Water of life' may be the semantic origin of whisky: water is the lifeblood of Scotch. It is the trilling burns, each with its own characteristics – an

expert can spot differences in two whiskies made a few hundred yards apart on opposite sides of a glen – that impart much of the unique qualities of Scotch. This wonderfully pure water is used to moisten barley before it goes to the malting floors, so that it sprouts, giving out a shoot a thumb-nail long. To aerate it, the sprouting barley is constantly turned, sometimes by hand, but more often today by a 'Saladin' machine which – and this is not always the case with mechanisation – does the job just as efficiently. The growth of the barley is halted by drying. The fires that dehydrate the barley are stoked with peat from the million-year-old deposits that are almost as inexhaustible as the abundant streams. The peat smoke – the delicious 'reek' which adds its own special aroma to the unpolluted Scottish air – permeates the barley with a flavour it retains through all subsequent processes. The dried malt is now ground, not too finely, and, in vast vats, on to it is poured hot, abundant quantities of that superb water. Mechanical stirrers agitate the mash and from it is drawn a sweetish liquid, the wort, which is cooled. In great containers yeast is added to this wort. The action of the yeast on the sugar in the wort sets up a violent fermentation, transforming the sugar into alcohol. The result is a sort of beer – the wash – with an alcohol strength of around 10 per cent.

Now the alcoholic wash is distilled. First it goes into a wash-still. This produces a fairly weak and impure spirit called 'low wines'. The next stage is to charge these into a second – or 'low wines' – still, and the product of this secondary distillation is what will become pure Scotch malt whisky. But not for a while. First comes the all-important maturation in oak casks. These may be actual sherry casks, but manifestly the supply of these is insufficient for a giant industry, and a majority will be wine-treated casks, a high proportion being imported – broken into their constituent staves – from the USA (see American whiskey). No one knows precisely what happens when spirit is matured in wood, but the effect is clear enough. The unwanted impurities in the spirit are dissipated into the air, and, in the instance

of Scotch, something from the pure air of Scotland gives special virtue to the whisky. By law, whisky may not be broached until it has been three years in cask, but most malt is matured much longer. Probably it does not achieve any additional merit beyond some twenty years.

Now comes the blending. The art of the blender is another factor in the mystery of Scotch whisky. Each major blend differs and the maintenance of a precise standard of quality and taste is the blender's function. (There are blends which vary wildly from batch to batch). On average a blend will comprise 50 per cent malt and 50 per cent grain whisky. This grain whisky is a much blander and simpler spirit than malt. It is rarely matured beyond the legal three year minimum and its function is to lighten the blend. In a good blend there will probably be around 30 individual malts, though in one instance, Black & White, over 60 malts are used, which both complicates the blender's task and makes for greater consistency from year to year. At the other extreme are blends which, quite legally, in order to economise, use just a tiny proportion of one or two good malts and fill up with grain. In the case of fine Scotch, under the blender's eye, the precise proportion of various malts and grain whiskies are mixed in vats in huge quantities and then transferred to casks for further maturing so that the whiskies may 'marry' completely. Thereafter, there is only filtration and bottling to be done before Scotch is ready for the markets of the world.

In the Cocktail and Mixed Drinks section of this book one or two of the less orthodox uses of Scotch are given. No more than with any of the other great spirits of the world is there a way in which they ought to be drunk. Drink Scotch the way you prefer it; in Scotland itself, outside distilling circles, the preferred additive is fizzy lemonade! Obviously, it is hardly sensible to drink a single malt other than neat or with a little water or soda (soda-water rouses the flavour of a spirit); but a blend may be taken with a wide range of mixers, if you prefer your Scotch other than with the little water that connoisseurs profess to be the only addition allowable.

Opposite Dalwhinnie Distillery, Inverness, is typical of most of Scotland's malt whisky distilleries in its remote isolation.
Top The malted barley, after grinding, is mixed with hot water in huge tuns. The sweetish liquid, or wort, thus produced, is then drawn off, and when yeast is added to it, it will produce the alcoholic wash from which Scotch is distilled.
Above Here the barley is being turned on the malting floor of a Scotch whisky distillery to ensure an even rate of sprouting. To a great extent this process is now mechanised.

Single malt is the product of a single distillery. **Blended malt** is the product of several distilleries, but is only composed of malt whisky. This may also be described as **straight malt**: in the trade it is called vatted (ie mixed in a vat) malt. The age on a single malt, if given, is the actual wood age of the spirit. In the case of blends–be they of straight malt or a blend of malt and grain–a given age refers to the youngest whisky in the blend. Only a minority of Scotch whiskies indicate an age and these are usually in the de luxe class. The better blends of commerce will have an average, undeclared, age of about six years.

Scotch enjoys some favour in medical circles, though I sometimes wonder how much this is based on patriotism, for Scots are very prominent in the profession. However, Scotch is not infrequently the only spirit doctors permit certain cardiac patients. Scotch is also said to be an excellent preventative of the queasiness induced by exotic holiday foods in strange places! But it is just because more discriminating people like it than they do any other spirit that Scotch reigns supreme amongst the world's great spirits wherever quality matters.

Bottom The sampling room of Talisker Distillery, Isle of Skye. The pure alcohol is run off from the still in its pure state, which is colourless.
Below The still house of Talisker Distillery.
Opposite Blending—vital to the Scotch whisky industry. Here a blender is seen 'nosing' samples of whisky: only the aroma interests him; he does not taste the spirit.

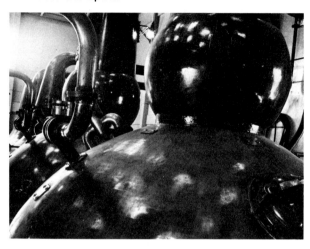

American whiskey

Including the recently unveiled American light whiskey, US law covers 30 types of American whisky. We can forget a good many of them, especially when one realises that the simple, unqualified term 'whiskey' may legally be applied to 20 per cent of a two-year-old distillation blended with 80 per cent neutral spirit. And whilst we are considering that end of the market, it should be remembered that 'moonshining', though past its heyday, means an annual accretion to US spirit consumption of anything up to 60 million gallons of illicit distillations. The authorities are uncovering a mere 3,000 stills a year compared with three-times that number a decade ago, but illegal production remains formidable, particularly in Kentucky.

Whilst American **Bourbon whiskey** is still a pretty small number in the British market, sales of it are rising—in common with other spirits. On the European continent, particularly in West Germany, it is becoming markedly more fashionable—German admiration for the USA is probably reflected here. Whether the latent anti-Americanism of the French will stop a large Gallic demand remains to be seen; French chauvinism certainly did not stop a tidal wave of Scotch embracing the country, but it might be argued that Scotland and France have a long history of amity (conveniently forgetting the Highlanders' brilliant victories at Waterloo) not always shared by the southern portion of the United Kingdom. I only raise this as a debating point: do international prejudices affect drinking patterns?

It was in what is now Kentucky, though then part of Virginia, that American's most famous whiskey, protected since 1964 by Act of Congress, was born in Bourbon County in 1789. In that year, in Georgetown—named for George III but an appropriate title since George Washington became first US President in 1789—the Rev Elijah Craig started a distillery. His product must have been excellent, since, of all names associated with American distilling, it was Bourbon that stuck. Sometimes erroneously employed as a generic description for American whiskey, Bourbon is clearly defined as being distilled from a mash containing not less than 51 per cent maize (corn), the distillate not exceeding 160 proof US (80 per cent alcohol), and must be matured in new casks. (This proviso has provided a constant flow of used casks for use in Scotland. They have soaked up some 4 gallons of whiskey apiece, and, after re-building, charring and wine-treatment, are admirable for storing Scotch.) But the comparatively low strength at which Bourbon is distilled (invariably below the maximum), the constituents of the mash, and the use of new casks, all combine to produce a whiskey which is decidedly high in flavour. For long, the American industry demanded the right to produce whiskey at a higher proof and, particularly, to store it for maturing in previously used casks which do not lose so much whiskey into the wood, and, more important, impart much less wood flavour to the spirit. The Americans claimed that they were at a disadvantage compared with Scotch and could not produce a whiskey which conformed as much to modern tastes as Scotch or Canadian whisky. Eventually they got their way and persmission was given to produce American light whiskey, distilled at very high proof and matured for four years in used casks. This

spirit was released to a not very expectant or excited world in 1972. It will be some time before the eventual destiny of light whiskey unfolds, but current indications are that most of the first release from bond has been going into American blends. Straight Bourbon certainly has not suffered from this incursion, nor have Scotch or Canadian imports. Bourbon is made in a number of states as well as Kentucky: Tennessee Bourbon enjoys a high reputation.

The other important American whiskey is **rye.** This is made under conditions similar to those pertaining to Bourbon, but the mash must consist of at least 51 per cent rye. It does not carry the prestige of Bourbon. In fact, colloquially, if incorrectly, the word 'rye' is often applied to Canadian whisky, as in 'rye and dry'. At least in Britain, this seems to have come to mean Canadian whisky and dry ginger ale. Just to confuse the issue, 'rye and dry' is often ordered with American (sweet) ginger ale.

Straight (unblended) Bourbon is the principal American whiskey encountered overseas. In the USA, the majority of whiskey sold is blended. **Blended Bourbon** or **blended rye** must contain 51 per cent of the type mentioned; if they do not, they may be labelled 'blended', but without mentioning Bourbon or rye. Brand names carry considerable significance; average drinkers grow to rely on a particular brand as being what they prefer in a particular price range. They do not necessarily know much about what type of whiskey it is. The other distinctive type of American whiskey is **corn,** made from at least 80 per cent maize. It may be aged in used casks, for a minimum two years. This is often sold at very high strength and has its devotees.

Canadian whisky

You may note that Canadian whisky does not carry the 'e'. This might be because Canadian whisky certainly owed its origin to the tide of Scottish settlers in the Dominion. Yet the two spellings of the word are of recent definition; until quite recently both were indiscriminately in use. The Royal Commission of 1909 which finally decided the vexed question of what constituted Scotch used 'whiskey' throughout its report.

Canadian whisky is mainly based on maize, with some wheat and malted barley. Continuous, not pot-still, distillation is the rule, and the result has affinities to both Scotch and rye. Without intending to be pejorative, I have previously described Canadian as a compromise whisky. It pleases drinkers of both Bourbon and Scotch, which may be why it outsells Scotch in a number of states in the USA. Two brands have good distribution in Britain, and Canadian whisky, of which the production is keenly supervised by governmental officials, is invariably of high quality; there is none of the 'jungle juice' which marks the lower end of the American whiskey scene. Canadian whisky is principally employed in the same way as American, ie for highballs, 'rye and dry', Manhattans, Old Fashioneds (see Cocktails).

Irish whiskey

The popularity of Irish coffee has done much to re-introduce people to this spirit, though in England it is not widely popular in other forms, whereas a century ago it was virtually the only style of whiskey drunk in England. It has a strong market in the USA, largely for reasons of ethnic nostalgia. It is certainly the oldest of whiskies. Nine hundred years ago whiskey of a sort was being made in Ulster. Northern Ireland is arguably the home of the finest Irish whiskey, **Old Bushmills liqueur** – known as 'Bush Black' – an aged and noble spirit demanding no additive or dilution.

In the Republic, the industry is in the hands of a combine who produce virtually all the brands sold there – a handful of well-known names. A great deal of Scotch is drunk in Eire and in the North.

Irish whiskey is customarily based on a mash of barley (only half being malted), wheat, rye, and, peculiar to Ireland, oats. Pot-stills are the rule. As there are only a few distilleries, not much blending is possible. By law, Irish whiskey is matured for seven years. This makes for smoothness, but the whiskey is basically a highly-flavoured one – an acquired taste, but rightly enjoying a place amongst the four notable whiskies of the world.

Opposite The still house of St John's Lane Distillery, Dublin. Irish whiskey was, a century ago, the only style of whiskey drunk in England. It has a large market in the USA today, and is certainly the oldest of whiskies, dating back as far as medieval times.

Above From left to right: the American Bourbon-based Southern Comfort; a well-known brand of Bourbon whiskey (Bourbon was 'born' in Kentucky in 1789); Canadian whisky, which is mainly based on maize; and the famous Scotch-whisky-based liqueur, Drambuie.

St John's Lane Distillery, Dublin, founded by James Power in 1791.

Other whiskies

In the past **Japanese whisky** was rather a joke, sometimes a pretty sick one. It is not today. Largely disappeared is the 'Ben Osaka' 'Mc Fujiyama' image, or my favourite description on a label: 'pressed from the finest Scottish grapes'. A tremendous amount of Scotch malt whisky is imported into Japan and blended with local distillations, greatly to their benefit and mainly without deception. The object is eventually to produce, not an imitation Scotch, but a distinctive Japanese whisky, with its own virtues, to stand on its own feet beside other distillations. Meanwhile, in Europe we are for some time likely to read more about Japanese whisky than to see it around the stores.

Quite tolerable whisky is made in numerous countries. Australia has been a considerable and excellent producer since distillation started in the shortages of World War I. But one must exercise considerable discretion. There remains a great deal of imitation Scotch, some of it local distillations blended with often immature malt, much of it terrible hooch candidly trying to foist itself off as the real thing, down to some clever (or hilarious) counterfeiting of famous brand packs.

Whisky-based brands

There are sundry proprietory drinks based on various whiskies. The best-known Scotch-based liqueur is certainly **Drambuie,** one of the world's great liqueurs. In Ireland, **Irish Mist** is comparatively modern, but claims to come from an ancient recipe, lost for centuries. A newcomer is **Irish Velvet,** a blend of Irish whiskey, coffee and sugar–instant Irish Coffee. All you do is add hot water and cream. From the USA we have the Bourbon-based **Southern Comfort,** becoming quite popular in Britain, powerful and, though here treated as a liqueur, in its homeland used more as a whiskey. Latterley there have been several widely-advertised 'Scotch' drinks based on malt whiskey blended with British wine. These are designed to attract fortified wine, not spirit, taxation, and contain only about 17 per cent alcohol (though labelled, quite correctly, as 31 proof spirit, which some people might conceivably misinterpret as 31 of actual alcohol). It is for you to judge whether their inexpensiveness is more apparent or real: equally, the flavour undertones of Scotch may be more manifest to you than to myself.

16

奉納 サントリーウィスキー株式会社

奉納 ★ サッポロビール

Japan is now producing distinctive whiskies which may currently owe much of their virtue to being blended into imported Scotch malt whisky, but which no longer pretend to be Scotch.

Japanese whisky—they prefer the Scottish to the American spelling of the word—is almost wholly consumed domestically, but export is commencing.

'Don't tell my mother I'm living in sin,
Don't let the old folks know;
Don't tell my twin that I breakfast on gin,
He'd never survive the blow.'
Sir A P Herbert

Hogarth's celebrated morality picture, 'Gin Lane',
epitome of the 'gin era' when the spirit—at that
time incredibly cheap—provided a palliative for
the horrors of 18th-century urban life and
became a serious health-hazard.

Gin

Gin is produced and drunk very extensively. It owes its name to its prime ingredient: via the French for juniper, *genièvre,* came the Dutch *jenever* (or *genever*). In the mid-16th century, when a medicinal spirit, flavoured with oil of juniper–whose salubrity has been recognised for a thousand years and more– was invented, it came to be called **genever** when it was copied commercially in about 1570. The spirit was brought to England a few years later and acquired sufficient popularity in such places as London, Portsmouth, Plymouth and Bristol for a few brewers to start distilling it. English distilling was in its infancy: the rich drank French brandy (illicitly when England and France were at war); rum from the West Indies was appearing; and there was some whiskey from Ireland, but most Englishmen drank ale, cider, or wine when they could afford it. By 1688, however, this new spirit, often called Hollands, as well as geneva, in recognition of its mother country, had a production of some half-million gallons, mainly in ports and notably in London. In this year of vital importance to the story of gin, James II lost his throne and retired to France. From Holland William III and his English consort and co-sovereign, Mary, arrived to rule England. It was co-incidental that King William came from the Low Countries, but one of his first Acts was to give a free rein to English distilling–which meant gin (a typical English corruption of geneva)–to ensure a market for copious English grain and to combat the smuggling of brandy from a hostile France. So far as London was concerned, control of distilling was vested in the livery company of the Distillers, whose Charter had been granted by Charles I. The founder was the remarkable Sir Theodore de Mayerne, physician to one French monarch and three successive English ones. The Distillers forbade the sale of unrectified (unpurified) spirit. Unfortunately, in due course Queen Anne, whilst continuing to encourage gin production, for some extraordinary reason revoked the Distillers' Charter, thereby releasing a deluge of inferior gin or rank spirit that was not technically gin at all.

By 1727 gin production was running at 5 million gallons; six years later London alone consumed 11 million gallons, and by 1743 a population of 6½ millions–a large proportion of them non-spirit drinkers–got through a (literally) staggering 18 million gallons of gin, quite apart from other intoxicants. Before that, seeing that the masses were greatly enjoying themselves–which governments tend to consider a 'bad thing'–and that they might be ruining their health (to which no one greatly objected) and, which was important, possibly losing their desire to toil for the benefit of their rulers, parliament passes a series of Gin Acts. Their object was both to reduce the consumption of gin, which did provide some relief from the horrors of 18th-

A gin palace in the 1870s, target of Mr Gladstone's unpopular Bill to cut down the number of public houses. The Bill was withdrawn.

century urban proletarian life, and to raise revenue. The inebriated mob had no intentions of being deprived of their tipple by equally inebriated parliamentarians. Abetted by many a crafty distiller and retailer, the Acts were evaded or simply flouted. Informers disappeared, witnesses went inexplicably blind and deaf, juries refused to convict. Legislative ineptitude compounded social chaos. Riot and mayhem prevailed and gin, much of it noxious, went on its horrific way. Not till the middle of the 18th century did some sanity come into the control of the gin trade, encouraging reputable distillers to lay the foundations of the modern industry, and a small abatement in the thirst for ardent spirit became apparent. From this gin era–epitomised in Hogarth's celebrated morality picture–a somewhat clouded image of gin was retained almost into our own times: even when gin had become universally esteemed, jokes about 'mother's ruin' persisted.

With the flowering of the Industrial Revolution, gin again came into the news. It was the target of the growing Temperance movement; its name was immortalised in the Victorian gin palaces. These were social focal points in all cities, oases of brightness and gaiety in acres of smoke-grimed dwellings. They played a notable role in the life of the community. The licensee was an important citizen, derided (and envied) by professional folk, admired and courted by his customers. The gin palaces were very popular–but not necessarily with the government. In the 1870s, Mr Gladstone decided the time had come to halve the number of public houses where people enjoyed themselves when they might have been working, in which they spent money which might be, in his liberal opinion, better invested. He did not succeed, though in those days the House of Lords considered itself the custodian of the welfare of the common man.

Above Whatever technological equipment may be perfected for the production of Scotch whisky, someone has to cut the peat—essential to the process.

Opposite, top The turning of the sprouting barley on the malting floor by hand is giving way to mechanical methods. Those are just as efficient as the more picturesque process traditionally identified with Scotch whisky, and are more economical.
Opposite, bottom The finished product, ready to drink.

I must not devote undue space to a single spirit, yet I do find gin's long story full of interest; it is closely woven into English social history. In the 1880s came a notable development. In response to a demand of which no record remains, some London distillers started to put out **unsweetened gin** in place of the variety of sweetish and cordial gins–akin to Dutch gin–which had hitherto been the vogue. The last of these to linger on was Old Tom, a pungent gin that has finally disappeared from the British scene but which is still produced in London for a few overseas markets, notably northern Finland. This unsweetened gin was the precursor of London dry gin. Meanwhile, gin was taking a social upturn. From far-flung posts of Empire returning governors brought home, along with loot and honours, a taste for drinking Indian quinine tonic water and gin. In the Royal Navy, which none dared criticise, officers drank gin with Angostura bitters, later known as pink gin. Undoubtedly this started as a health precaution on tropical stations, but became a social pattern dear to the Senior Service. Social trend-setters courageously adopted the American habit of ingesting gin cocktails, though not until after World War I did the extraordinary 'cocktail age'–which gave social approval to gin–blast through the tiny, but influential, world of the 'bright young things'.

Today, London dry gin is the type most used.

Dutch gin has its followers, and not only in Holland, but its heavy flavour makes it unsuitable for mixed drinks. It has lost a lot of the popularity it enjoyed in Britain pre-World War Two. Another distinctive type of gin is Plymouth, taking its name from that city. It was once very much associated with the Royal Navy and with pink gin, but today it is less aromatic and, particularly in the West Country, is used for the usual gin drinks. I have had difficulty in describing **Plymouth gin,** so I asked the owners, Coates & Co (a subsidiary of an American combine) to do it for me. They say it is, 'dry, but soft–with a unique formula achieving a fine balance between traditional gins and the currently popular London Gin, thus satisfying Gin-and-tonic drinkers as well as those who favour additives like Vermouth or Angostura Bitters.'

'Steinhaeger' is a German style of gin, from Westphalia, owing more in flavour to Dutch than to London Dry Gin. It is, like Geneva, usually drunk as a schnapps–neat and heavily chilled.

London dry gin does not carry a geographic connotation (though the French maintain it does). However, it is widely accepted that it is in London the finest of all dry gin is made, and nowhere is this more obvious than in the United States, great importers of gins from London and where the principal US-distilled gin (Gordon's) is controlled from London.

Above The distillery and warehouses of De Kuyper and Zoon at Schiedam, near Rotterdam. *Right* A modern distillery, though belonging to a firm established in 1740, Booth's Ltd. At the back are three flavouring stills; to the left two rectifying stills, and on the right are condensers.

There are an enormous number of London dry gins: on the British market there are several dozen. But it is generally agreed that no more than some five in fairly general commerce rate as absolutely first rate. The idea that 'they are all the same' is prevalent concerning gin, even amongst quite well-informed persons. This is incorrect. Gin is an artificially flavoured spirit; the formulae used by the principal brand-owners are secret to them. The proportions of botanical ingredients, and even the number, vary considerably. Even the methods of manufacture differ in marked particulars. Some lesser gins are made by short cut processes that do not produce the ideal end-product. In many countries there are some terrible spirits that may technically be gin (i.e. contain a trace of juniper) but which are best avoided. Often these have misleading labels: the warning I posted about whiskey substitutes applies also to gin in some parts of the world.

The best London dry gin starts as a good, but still unrefined, spirit. It may be based on cane (molasses) or grain. (Grain spirit carries an irreducible flavour of its own and thus some authorities aver that fine cane spirit is a cleaner base for gin.) This is re-distilled – rectified – by which means it is totally purified and all undesirable congeners cast aside. To the particular brand recipe this very pure spirit is then flavoured with juniper, coriander and a very small quantity of other botanical ingredients. Orris root, cassia bark and angelica are frequently, but not necessarily, employed.

Gin may be claimed to be the only spirit in wide-spread use that has, as an inherent part of its character, a flavouring which has therapeutic merit. Oil of juniper is a well-known diuretic – that is to say, it can act beneficially in aiding the elimination of uric acid and the like. Personally, I believe from experience that gin is a beneficent spirit, but to be rewarded by its virtues it should ideally be taken only with water – possibly with fresh fruit juice. But I will not proceed too deeply into the field of drinking medicinally; rather, let us consider gin's social position. This will be apparent from the number of classic mixed drinks (see Cocktail chapter) which are gin-based, even if there are nowadays variations on them that employ rival spirits.

Not for nothing did the late André Simon, who did not care for gin himself, describe it as 'the purest of all spirits.'

Above right Sir Felix Booth, greatest distiller of his day (1780–1850), played a major part establishing the supremacy of London gin.
Right An old photograph of the most ancient gin still in London, dating from Booth's establishment in 1740 of the Old Red Lion Distillery, London. The still has now been demolished.

Tommy Langley, head bartender at Jules Bar, Jermyn Street, London, and a member of the Council of the United Kingdom Bartenders Guild, mixes a formidable 'Bloody Mary'. On the counter are tins containing American 'Bloody Mary' and 'Bloody Bullshot' mixes, though he is not employing them. The author opines that these mixes (you add the vodka and ice) from the USA are the only permissible ones: he can't abide other ready-made mixes for sours, Collins and the like.

Vodka

As gin made a gradual change from the traditional highly-flavoured liquor to the delicate rectified spirit with which most of us associate it, so did vodka change. But here the alteration was almost dramatically quick – and modern. So we have to be quite clear what we are talking about when we speak of vodka. Decidedly there are two basic types. One I will call, though that is not its official name, Slavonic, and the other Anglo-Saxon. Slavonic vodka is essentially a product of Russia and Poland, in one of which countries it was invented centuries ago: I am not saying which country, since the nations' histories are much intertwined. These traditional vodkas are, in their export form, lightly-flavoured matured grain spirits of good quality. In my opinion, they are best drunk as tradition demands – very cold, neat, straight down the hatch, accompanied by the tastiest nibbles of food you can afford, and are wonderful with caviar, or smoked salmon if you are not rich but like extravagance. Though we don't see many of them abroad, the Russians produce a huge variety of vodkas, and the word is virtually synonymous with strong spirits rather as schnapps is in Germany. A report I saw on a Russian vodka factory listed over thirty distinct types of vodka with a flavour range embracing chocolate and cayenne pepper. (The Poles also export a 'pure spirit' which, at 140 proof, must be the strongest spirit normally available in Britain. To be treated with great caution: it is really too powerful to drink undiluted.) Two special vodkas are **Wisniowka** (sharply cherry-flavoured) and **Zubrowka** (tinged green with a mildly aromatic herb.)

Vodka is part of the way of life in Russia and Poland. Before the 1914 war, from a single distillery in Moscow came one million bottles of vodka a day. When war came, the Czar banned vodka production, and the post-war communist regime maintained this ban until 1925. It was then reintroduced as a state monopoly, but the years of prohibition had established a pattern of illicit distilling which still plagues the country. Also established was an alcoholism problem and every now and then the Soviet press publishes diatribes against this anti-social disease.

For a long time, vodka – which can be translated affectionately as 'little water' – was the standard drink of Russians, Poles, Finns, many of the Balkan peoples, and as far East as Persia. Its popularity faded the closer one got to the Rhine, the North Sea and the Mediterranean. It took a drinking revolution to make vodka – albeit of a different style – a global product. Which brings us to what I call 'Anglo-American' vodka.

The vodka phenomenon is worth tracing in a little detail, as it is a classic example of the combination of good luck and good promotion making success. Having acquired the rights to the name **Smirnoff**

'I was the mainstay of the Public Library until I discovered Smirnoff.'

The effect is shattering

SMIRNOFF VODKA

'Accountancy was my life until I discovered Smirnoff.'

The effect is shattering

SMIRNOFF VODKA

from the exiled family who had reputedly once been the world's richest industrial clan, a Ukranian hopefully started production in the US in 1934. There simply was not any real demand for vodka. Five years later, through the enthusiasm of its president, John G Martin, who was born in England, the respected but then small Heublein company of Hartford, Connecticut, took over the brand's manufacture and sale. They got rid of 6,000 cases a year.

John Martin retained his faith. One happy day, in the Cock 'n Bull Tavern, Los Angeles, he was playing around with the ideas for a vodka drink with Jack Morgan, the tavern's proprietor. They came up with a mixture of vodka, ginger beer (a rather exotic English product in California) and lime juice. They christened it **Moscow Mule** and launched it. By 1947, the trend-setting West Coast smart set were crazy for Moscow Mules: American drinkers are highly susceptible to examples set by show-biz personalities in particular. The Moscow Mule really took off, quickly followed by Screwdriver (vodka and fresh orange juice), and then the Bullshot. Vodka within a few years very seriously rivalled gin, and eventually overtook it in the States, though there is now an indication that gin is successfully fighting back.

This drinking revolution made little immediate impact elsewhere. Not until around 1955 did vodka start to move in Britain, and then it was in Scotland. Some say it was because a lot of Poles settled there after the war, but I doubt this, for they would not find a great deal of joy in this Anglo-Saxon style of vodka. And, anyway, it was essentially the young drinkers' drink at first. More likely vodka moved because Scotch was by no means yet in abundant supply after the wartime dearth, and also that young Scots wanted to show they were independent of their father's prejudice in favour of the national spirit. When the vodka vogue spread south, again it was the young who took to it. It also had a rather female following. To some extent the latter is still true, but vodka continues to grow strongly in popularity and it is obvious that not only are more and more men drinking it but it is the regular spirit of a much more mature male and female consumer group than was previously the case. There has been a proliferation of brands, and it is a signal of vodka's success that no longer is it simply a product but the more discerning drinkers are demanding a brand of it by name. In this field there are two leaders, the Smirnoff which made the fashion, and **Cossack,** which has enjoyed phenomenal success.

Some of vodka's popularity may be due to certain notions (I was almost going to say fallacies) that have grown up concerning it. It is said to be less fattening than other spirits and less conducive to hangovers: this can only be true in that the great majority of vodka drunk in the UK is produced at 65·5 proof instead of the usual 70 proof of other spirits (see glossary regarding proof). It is also said to 'show' less than other spirits but this is largely illusory: if you're tight, it'll show and you'll smell of drink. But it is, of course, a very clean spirit. Vodka (the style we're talking about) starts as an already fine spirit, which is then purified further by careful filtration through a special form of charcoal. The whole object of 'Anglo-American' vodka is to get a spirit which is as near flavourless as it is possible to make one. The great virtue of this vodka is certainly that you can mix it with anything you like–tonic, cola, squashes, vermouth, etc. It won't impart any flavour to the mix, only give it a kick, and this is what some drinkers want. When dealing with cocktails and mixed drinks, you can take it that almost any gin drinks I mention can have vodka instead–though personally I don't relish the variation–and in the instance of Dry Martini I have evolved a special variation designed specifically for vodka. There are a handful of mixed drinks strongly identified with vodka alone.

Rum

The rummiest thing about rum is its name! Most famous spirituous products have names with easily traceable origins. Not so with rum. Quite likely it derived from 'Rumbustion' (the 'rumbullion' of seafaring Devonians) which once meant both 'uproar' and 'strong spirit'. Equally, it could be a corruption of the Spanish *ron* (French *rhum*) itself probably coming from the Latin *saccharum* (sugar)–for indubitably the Spaniards were cultivating cane in the West Indies, and distilling from it, before anyone else.

In the 17th century a spirit distilled from molasses was known as 'kill devil' by the slaves to whom it was given to keep them going in the appalling conditions under which they lived and worked. At the beginning of the 18th century, something called rum had found its way to England and was beginning to usurp the monopoly held by brandy in the punches beloved by the better-off. The enforced maturing in cask whilst the spirit sailed to England would greatly have improved it. In the sugar-producing islands and South American mainland of the Caribbean and South Atlantic, rum was widely produced and obviously plantation owners would try to improve its quality. Prior to the foundation of the United States, rum was immensely popular in the British North American colonies, for whisky distilling had not started, though the Dutch had produced some spirit (presumably a form of gin) when they held New Amsterdam (New York). New England was a major rum-producing area, from imported molasses, until quite recent times: there is still a small production enjoying a rather special reputation.

'Drink and the devil had done for the rest—
Yo-ho-ho and a bottle of rum!'
Treasure Island Robert Louis Stevenson

Here sailors on board a man of war are being
given an extra ration of rum to celebrate Queen
Victoria's jubilee.

Rum had a particular sea-faring connection, and still has in many ports. It became the Nelson's 'blood of the Royal Navy,' but, when Britain virtually gave up having ships in favour of simply having admirals, the traditional rum issue was stopped, to the horror of nearly everyone except the Temperance movement.

We now come to another spirituous dichotomy. There is precious little in common between the old rum of the Navy and what a party of youngsters mean by rum when they go into a pub, except that both are technically rums. In fact, the youngsters may not ask for rum at all: they'll ask for, say, 'Bacardi and . . .' They might even be unaware that they've asked for a type of rum, nor know that they have named a brand.

Rum was defined in British law in 1904 as spirit distilled from sugar cane in sugar-producing countries. At that time rum was a distinctively pungent spirit. It was almost invariably dark, or darkish yellow. Lately we have seen a great change and a firm separation of rum into dark and white.

White rum has long been produced—it is the first and natural distillation from molasses—but mostly this was drunk where it was made, unmatured, with local additives like fruit juices or coconut milk. There was little demand for it overseas. For export the rum would need flavouring with a concentrate,

and darkening with burnt sugar. It might naturally be rich if distilled by pot-still, though it would not naturally be dark—for all distillates are originally white, whatever their flavour. (Though spirits pick up some colour from wood during maturing—quite a lot of colour if the casks are charred and/or wine-treated as for Scotch—all coloured spirits need additional colouring to adjust them to the brand's requirements. Colour, or lack of it, in spirits has no effect on taste.

White rum came into the broader field via Cuba. In pre-Castro Havana, a sort of Caribbean Paris for many Americans, the tourists imbibed large quantities of white rum-and-coke, thus combining an alien spirit with their preferred mixer. This was known as a **Cuba Libre,** though Cuba was no more free than it is today—just differently controlled. The smarter folk drank **Daiquiri** cocktails, an invention said to have occurred when, at the nickel-mine of that name, in Oriente province, expatriate Americans were reduced to drinking a mixture of local rum, local lime and local sugar syrup. The Daiquiri cocktail became fashionable with Americans when they flocked to Cuba not only for its freewheeling life style but for good alcohol, which their own government endeavoured to deny them from 1919-33. The Daiquiri has endured: the Cuba Libre has been revived.

'Fill ev'ry glass, for wine inspires us
And fires us
With courage, love and joy.
Women and wine should life employ.
Is there aught else on earth desirous?'
The Beggar's Opera John Gay

Bacchus, traditionally god of wine. Wine must be the most ancient alcoholic beverage. Very early in man's history fortuitous fermentation of wild grapes led to the cultivation of the wine and purposeful pressing to obtain juice, thus making wine of the most natural kind. Knowledge of the merits of maturing came much later: wines of yore were certainly drunk young and often with herbal additives to mellow their brashness. Their use was almost as much ritual as social or restorative.

'Go thy way, eat thy bread with joy, and drink thy wine with a merry heart'.
Ecclesiastes, ii, 7

Diluted molasses, principal ingredient of rum, in full fermentation.

Spanish holidays are said to have played a part in the recent interest shown in white rum, or it may be simply that youngsters are looking for a new spirit. From virtually nil, light white rum now accounts for about a third of the UK rum sales and its percentage increases yearly. There are plenty of brands now available, and more coming on to the shelves all the time. It is still very much the youngster's drink, serving a market similar to that for vodka a decade ago. My crystal decanter doesn't tell me whether white rum will repeat vodka's success and move up market; for all one can guess, today's young drinkers may move back to the traditional whisky, gin and brandy of British drinking—or is there another spirit waiting for discovery?

Apart from rather special rums—pot-distilled and mainly island-bottled—production is now by patent still. A mash is made of molasses, by-product of the production of cane sugar, and water. Natural yeasts, plus special strains, cause the residual sugar in the molasses to ferment. The resultant alcohol wash is distilled in Coffey stills. This method allows the distiller to draw off more or less flavour from the wash as he requires. Generally speaking, the distillate will be very lightly flavoured. For **dark rum,** a highly refined distilled sugar distillate will be added. Colour will be adjusted to the degree associated with particular brands. For the British market, the spirit must be matured for the required three years minimum. The white rum will then have gained a little colour, and, to conform with the current growing demand for absolutely white rum, this must be de-coloured by elaborate filtering. This is a summary of typical modern rum distillation: manifestly, different firms have their own methods in matters of detail. White rums are tending to become very light indeed; some are almost flavourless. There is considerable variation in quality and price. As opposed to fine dark rums, virtually all white rum is taken with fairly highly flavoured additives; this irons out the difference. Traditional dark rums are a superb base for punch, particularly hot punch.

Brandy

Grape brandy is a phrase employed to distinguish brandy distilled from grape but not qualifying as Cognac, or the less common but splendid Armagnac. A huge amount of grape brandy is made in France and is increasingly to be seen in Britain. It is usually a distillation of no great consequence as to quality, though quite palatable in fancy drinks; but on no account to be confused with Cognac. Grape brandy is unlikely to have been matured for more than three years. It may even be, and this should be reflected in the price, of lower than normal strength. Sound brandy comes from South Africa, Cyprus, Australia, Spain, Greece, Italy and Germany–and other countries. German brandy is perhaps the one making the biggest export push, and is enjoying a growing reputation. Some of these national brandies have distinctive qualities and a number tend to be highly caramelised to induce a smoothness not inherent in the distillation. I think one particularly notices this in Spanish and Greek brandies, which seem to taste much better in their homelands than in Britain. In Britain, to be described as a brandy, a spirit must come from a grape base: it need not necessarily be from wine, as we understand it, since a reconstituted 'wine' from residue of pressed grapes will suffice. It may still be called brandy if it is subsequently flavoured with something else, but grape must be at the base of it.

The origin of the word is almost certainly from the Dutch *brandewijn,* meaning 'burned wine'; that is to say, distilled wine. At one time, ante-dating fine spirits, wine was sometimes crudely distilled to produce weak spirit that would nonetheless last better than the original rather poor wine. The notion of fortifying with alcohol for the same purpose came later. We probably owe the ancient term 'low wines' (still used to describe the first distillation in making Scotch) to this practice. You may remember that in writing on gin I explained how the Distillers Company of the City of London proscribed the sale of such 'low wines' and insisted they be further distilled. The Dutch were indubitably Europe's first commercial distillers of potable alcohol on any considerable scale. Three centuries or more ago the English used the term 'brande-wine' for any spirits; this became 'brandywine' and was shortened to 'brandy'.

To revert to brandy from grapes. Though every wine-producing country copiously produces brandy (California makes more than France), one country and one district of that country have become synonymous with superior, or superb, brandies.

Cognac's pre-eminence in brandy owes its source to 15th century efforts to produce 'burned wine' from the fresh, light wines of the Charente region of south-west France, with the twin objects of reducing the volume for export and preserving the beverage. This region, somewhat north of Bordeaux, was

Below left The Martell bottling plant.
Below right Stacking freshly filled new casks of

Hine Cognac in a recently built *chai* in Jarnac.
Bottom A receiving warehouse at Martell & Co.

Cultivation of the grape today covers a wide
horticultural spectrum—from fully mechanised
methods with high-trained, widely-spaced vines,
to the purely manual care of low-pruned,
densely-planted vines. A worker in the Loire
Valley of France tends the vines with loving and
meticulous care.

long an English fief and wine had been coming thence for a very long time indeed. It was not until the 17th century that a distiller captured the elegantly-phrased 'soul of the wine' by employing a second distillation. This was Cognac's real origin. Also, there appeared to be something mysterious about the wines grown in the district. They were very ordinary wines – but they produced the most wonderful brandy. A scientific approach to this was made over a century ago, jointly by a geologist and a wine and spirit expert. The former had decided ideas on what soil should produce the best wine for brandy distillation. He was right. Wherever he said conditions were best, that soil did produce the most suitable wine. From this came severe legal definitions of the sundry areas into which the district is divided: Grande Champagne, Petite Champagne, Borderies, Fins Bois, Bons Bois, and Bois Ordinaries. There are some other districts technically pertaining to Cognac but this would confuse the issue. Only brandy from the clearly designated Cognac region, centring on the towns of Cognac and Jarnac, may carry the prestigious name under French law, and this is protected in most countries. The use of the word champagne is a trifle confusing. It simply means 'field' (cultivated area) from the Latin *campania* and has absolutely no connection with the celebrated wine. **Fine Champagne,** a term to be seen on bottles of high quality Cognac, means that the contents are a blend of spirit from the Grande and Petite Champagnes, with not less than 50 per cent of the former: Fine Champagne is not a district in itself. **Grande Champagne,** unblended with spirit from other districts, is the finest of all. The name Cognac, and the use of the descriptions Grande and Fine Champagne, are carefully restricted under French law. Other descriptions for grades of Cognac – Three Star, Vieille Cognac, VSOP (Very Special Old Pale), etc have no force of law behind them. Their use is at the discretion of the brand-owners: it is the reputation of these which is the buyer's sole guarantee. Most important brands also have registered brand names for some or all of their grades.

Whilst we are on this subject, I had best dispose of the 'Napoleon' myth. It is not illegal to put the magic word on a bottle of modern brandy, but it has absolutely no meaning in itself. The only true **'Napoleon' Cognac** in existence is Lucien-Foucauld Fine Champagne Napoleon 1811. A cask of this was presented to the Emperor on the birth of his son, the ill-fated King of Rome. A large quantity of the same spirit was eventually shipped to England and contemporary bottles had an Imperial 'N' on a seal. A bottle is a rare collector's piece, yet the contents would either be undrinkable or very poor. (Some reputable firms put out a 'Napoleon' quality, but it is much more important to note whether it is a Grande or Fine Champagne than to be seduced by the Bona-part of the title!) Frequently, the use of the word is an unjustified pretension.

The wine from which Cognac is made is not matured: a few people keep it for drinking locally, but they are frankly considered eccentric. As soon as the wine is made, it is ready for distilling, and this commences immediately. Wine is stored in sealed concrete containers so that air may not get to it, for the distilling period may last well into the following year. There is still a cottage industry aura around the business: some farmers both grow vines, press their vintage and distil, selling the product to the great brandy houses. Others only make wine, which they take to commercial distillers who buy it and sell the resultant spirit. Some brandy houses own vineyards and distil; others only distil or only make wine. Some important firms do none of these things, but buy the best brandy they can for their own *chais* – of which more presently. They will have their regular suppliers as well as dealing in the open market for spirit. It is at the same time a mixed commerce and a closely controlled one.

Whether it be individual distillers or giant distillery, the process is exactly the same, though some may lean more heavily on modern aids than the farmer-distiller of whom I know, who judges the heat of his stills by the moment a blob of sealing-wax stuck to them melts! Only quite small stills are used, their pattern regulated and unchanged for generations. The first distillation produces a *broulli*, which might be described as 'low wines', with an alcoholic strength of about 28 per cent. The second distillation is known as the *bonne chauffe*, and between the two stills is a *chauffe-vin*, an ingeniously economical device – product of thrifty French husbandry – which uses the still's heat to warm the new wine, thus saving fuel. The second distillation produces a spirit that must not exceed 72 per cent alcohol. This ensures that a good deal of flavour is brought off from the wine.

The Cognac then is filled into casks and placed in the *chais*, which are ground-level cellars having some affinity to the *bodegas* of Spain. The casks are made from Limousin oak from adjacent forests. Earth-floored and well ventilated, some *chais* are of great antiquity. They remain remarkably cool even in the hot local summers, but the annual loss by evaporation is 3 per cent on average. This loss rejoices in the lovely name the Angel's Share.

Once a year, at stock-taking, the evaporation will be made up by topping up casks with brandy from an earlier vintage, thus building up long average wood age. At the end of the line, as it were, will be casks holding Cognac with a wood age of perhaps as much as fifty years. This will not improve further. Superb Cognac of this age will be put into glass vessels where it may be kept indefinitely without change of character, and it is used in small quantities to perfect the finest grades.

All Cognac in normal commerce is thus a blend from different years. Cognac is, therefore, not sold with a stated age. With the better brands you can take the very rough rule that Three Star will be an average five years in wood, and VSOP around twenty. Costlier grades will be up to forty years. But there is no law about this. I would re-emphasise that the name of the producer and, in costlier grades, the type of Cognac, are the important factors for the buyer. Nor, in this context—and the same applies to other spirits—should the words 'liqueur' or 'de luxe' ever be read in isolation: they are without legal significance and only have validity if reinforced by other information.

In France there is no such thing as a vintage Cognac: it is forbidden to put a date on a bottle. However, a Cognac shipped to Britain a year after the vintage from which it was distilled, and bottled in the UK after long maturing, may carry the date of that vintage. It should also indicate other facts including the date of bottling, for it is the cask-age that counts: Cognac, like any other spirit, does not improve in bottle. Nor, securely and imperviously sealed, will they deteriorate in normal conditions, unless exposed to sunlight. Vintage Cognac is unusual today. I lately came across a cask of Hine Grande Champagne 1948 which had since lain forgotten (oddly enough) in an old wine company's City of London cellars. It had lost some strength. But it tasted the nearest thing to spirituous nectar I know.

South from Cognac, in the proximity of Toulouse, lies the home of the other notable French brandy, **Armagnac.** Production is only a quarter that of Cognac, and the brandy is greatly appreciated by French connoisseurs. A higher proportion of the annual production of Armagnac than that of Cognac is drunk in France, and consequently less is exported. Armagnac is made by a single distillation and thus it requires much more ageing than other fine spirits—twenty years is quite common and the finer varieties are much older.

Armagnac tends to be more highly flavoured than Cognac and is distinctively different. Only the better grades are exported, the lesser ones going to make good brandy-based liqueurs and cordials, so it is a liqueur and, unlike ordinary Cognacs, wasted if used with additives or for the sundry mixed brandy drinks to which I refer in the appropriate section.

True liqueur Cognac (or Armagnac) is best taken in a balloon glass that should not be ornate nor vulgarly over-sized, but plain, thin, and should fit comfortably into the hand so that the exquisite aroma may be gently coaxed from the aged spirit. The glass should not be artificially heated. Indeed, some experts contend that the glass should actually be chilled: their theory is that a brandy settling on this releases its bouquet more caressingly.

A 19th-century print showing Wallachians distilling Slivovitz. This spirit, made from plums, is traditionally associated with Yugoslavia, though sometimes made elsewhere.

Absinthe drinkers in a Paris café. Absinthe, now outlawed because of its damaging effects, was the traditional drink of the literary and artistic circle in Paris during the late 19th century.

Another French brandy made from grapes is **marc,** and that produced from the fermented residue of Burgundy wine grape pressings is esteemed in some circles, though I find a liking for this tinged with inverted snobbery. (The Italian equivalent is **grappa** and the German **trester.**) Most marc, as understood in France, is unmatured grape spirit of poor quality.

Despite its vinous origin, the word brandy is often loosely applied to other spirits, such as **apple brandy** as a description of Calvados, the American apple jack. Calvados, distilled in Normandy from cider, is decidedly rough until it has achieved immense wood age; it can then be delicious, and rather expensive.

Cherry brandy is a delightful drink, based on grape brandy and flavoured with cherries, and usually slightly over half the strength of grape brandy, but it is possibly no more a brandy than sloe gin is a gin (dealt with under Liqueurs and Cordials).

Broadly referred to as brandies are:

Slivovitz, made from plums, particularly associated with Yugoslavia, though produced in Austria and in Balkan countries. In Alsace and Germany, this is called **Quetsch.**

Kirsch is at best a true distillation from cherries (not a cherry-flavoured brandy), including some crushed stones to give piquancy.

In South America **Pisco** is very widely used: it may be a type of grape brandy; though often classed as an aguardiente (see below).

Some other spirits

If you've visited some border states in the USA, you may have found them drinking **tequila**: it is enjoying a certain vogue. This is the national spirit of Mexicans and reflects their reputedly fiery temperament. It is a distillation in the *aguardiente* (fire-water) category. It comes from the fermented sap of the *agave,* a cactus-type plant, from which is produced *pulque,* the national alcoholic beverage: this is the base for the distillate *mescal,* which has hallucinatory qualities. Tequila is a refined form of mescal. About the only way non-Mexicans can drink it is as a 'Margarita'.

The word **aquavit** (the derivation is obvious) covers a huge range of spirits of various flavours as drunk in Scandinavia and Germany. It can mean different things to different people in different places; similarly Akavit.

Equally broad in definition is **arrack** (*raki, rakia*) of which the best is held to be made in the Far East from distilled toddy (fermented palm sap). Other sources are grapes, dates, coconuts, milk. It comes in various flavours, often aniseed, which makes it a form of pastis.

Pastis is the generic name (you will recognise Pernod and Ricard) for French aniseed-flavoured spirits which have replaced the outlawed absinthe: the latter, made in a few countries, contains oil of wormwood. Pastis-type drinks are widely popular; they are known as *ouzo* in Greece and *ojen* in Spain.

35

Wines

In 1972, a Mr Mario Ruspoli paid £4661 for a bottle (Jeroboam) of Château Mouton Rothschild 1870.

I shall now try to compress into a few thousand words of good sense that which one *basically* needs to know of wine, a subject on which not only is a vast amount written, but about which a lot of high-falutin nonsense is also disseminated.

There are very few countries that do not produce some wine. Where grapes can grow, wine will be made. World production is around 3,500 million gallons a year: of this the late André Simon said that 2 per cent can be classed a quality wine.

There are scores of strains of wine grapes (*vitis vinifera*), carefully selected over the centuries so that they have become separated from eating grapes. They have one important common factor: a natural yeast appears on them as they ripen. When, by pressing, this yeast mingles with the sugar in the juice, fermentation commences. Traditionally, pressing is performed by gay peasants jumping around in vats. This is still practised, but, for all it retains a picturesque element, wine is now an industry. It is more practical and economical to press by sundry mechanical means of varied sophistication.

White wine is produced from either black or white grapes or a mixture of both, the juice being quickly run off. Red wine is made from black grapes and the skins remain during fermentation of the juice to give colour. Rosé wine is properly made by retaining some red grape skins during fermentation, or it may be a mélange of red and white wine. Sparkling wines are at best made by keeping the carbon dioxide produced during secondary fermentation. Poor sparkling wines may be artificially carbonated. Semi-sparkling wines (*pétillant*) keep a proportion only of this gas. Carbon dioxide is produced in large quantities during all fermentation; for still wines it is allowed to escape.

Dry wines are made by allowing the yeast to consume all the sugar during fermentation. For sweet wines, either fermentation will be stopped before the sugar has been consumed, or the natural sugar content will be so high that, at a certain stage, sufficient alcohol will have been produced to kill the yeast, leaving a sweet alcoholic liquor. This is an extreme simplification, and anyone interested in home winemaking (a growth industry in Britain) will know there are many complications. In commercial vinification there are also varied methods for aiding production which are too complicated for these pages and some of which large scale winemakers might not necessarily wish to be publicised.

Wine may be drunk as soon as it is made: witness the new Beaujolais which has become rather a smart drink lately. However, wine really requires some maturing, in wood, or, for special wines, in bottle. Wine is a living thing, unless, for mass market consumption, it be pasteurised and rendered inert.

A director of Christie's wine department taking a sale of fine wines.

Wine tasting in progress before a sale of old wines at Christie's, London.

France

Wine is produced all over France except the northern coasts. Some of it is dreadful, and is even turned into industrial alcohol. The French drink a lot of terrible wine. They also produce the world's finest red wines, and, more arguably, the finest whites; certainly the best dry whites. To the regret of French connoisseurs, most of the very best French wines are exported. Now, world demand exceeds supply and prices are becoming absurd. However, sound, as opposed to great, French wines remain within the price range of many drinkers.

Bordeaux red

The British gave this the name **Claret,** a corruption of *clairet,* probably a mixture of red and white wine sent to England when the area belonged to the English crown, and now descriptive of a local light wine of no distinction. Bordeaux wines have long been bedevilled by the notorious classification of 1855, a far from comprehensive list made for a Paris exhibition. This divided the châteaux (vineyards) into 1st growth (*1er cru*), 2nd to 5th growth, exceptional growths, and sub-classifications, with further division by commune (St Emilion, Paulliac, etc.) It only dealt with the major districts of Médoc and Sauternes, ignoring the important Graves. It managed to relegate Mouton Rothschild to 2nd growth. A result has been to place so much emphasis on 1st to 5th *Crus* that it has become a widespread and fallacious snobbism to denigrate any châteaux not so classified. Several abortive efforts have been made to bring out a more sensible classification, but the 1855 list still stands. Of course, it gives a guide to some remarkable wines, but it tends, by inference, to do less than justice to others almost as good. Ignore it, I suggest.

So how does the ordinary drinker assess a claret? Remember that the words 'Château' and 'Château-bottled' (*mise en bouteilles au château*) are not the same. Without the latter on the label, the wine will have come from the vineyards of the château stated – to confuse the issue, not every vineyard literally has a château – but it may have been bottled (a) in France by a factor, or (b) overseas. The order of precedence, and often of quality, for a named wine is (1) château-bottled, (2) bottled in France, (3) bottled overseas. (A few great wines are only château-bottled or bottled in France). Next comes the district. Médoc, St Emilion, Pomerol, Graves, and the sub-divisions Paulliac, Margaux, Pessac, St Estèphe, St Julien, Cantenac-Margaux, and Listrac are the names most likely, but not exclusively, to be seen on good red wines. Now the question of year. I have strong feelings that vintage charts are misleading; rather to take a better name of a 'poor' year then an unknown one from a 'good' vintage is my personal rule. A respected château will not give a vintage to a bad wine. A non-vintage wine – a blend from different vintages – if coming from an excellent source will probably be better than a vintage wine of unknown provenance. Obviously, the ideal is a famous château-bottled vintage wine – but let us be practical. Also, there is a proliferation of little known but splendid châteaux to be considered. Only experience and luck can guide you thither, or the unbiased and informed advice of a knowledgeable wine merchant – a dying breed, yet still to be found. For a British-bottled wine, another important factor is the shipper. Again, experience will prove to you that certain names are particularly reliable. This applies to blended 'brand name' wines which I shall deal with separately. All these general considerations apply throughout the wine-buying field.

I must here deal as succintly as possible with the question of *Appellation Contrôlée*. This involves complicated regulations under French law protecting specific wine names – Bordeaux, Bourgogne, Pouilly, etc – and laying down the quantities that may be sold under certain regionally descriptive labels. It has obviated earlier abuses in naming French wines, but has proved far from perfect. It has no force except for wine bottled in France, each country having – or not having – its own wine laws. As I write, moves are afoot to bring in agreed regulations for all Common Market countries, and this will eventually affect wines sold in Britain – and may produce some headaches for commercial producers of British wines (qv). But at present the Germans have their own complex and stringent laws, whilst the Italians are endeavouring to introduce control into their previously anarchic and adulteration-menaced industry, while the French are taking a second look at Appellation Contrôlée. It may be some time before a practical EEC policy on wine labelling fructifies.

Though not very widely known outside France, perhaps potentially of more real interest to intelligent wine-drinkers than appellation contrôlée is VDQS – *vin délimité de qualité supérieur.* Here *supérieur* is a qualitative and not a topographical term. But there are plenty of sound wines that do not qualify for either AP or VDQS designation: those are your personal bargains.

Commanderie Du Bontemps of Médoc (Bordeaux) ceremonially tour a vineyard.

Bordeaux white

The most likely Appellation Contrôlée names encountered in good white Bordeaux wines are Barsac (very sweet), Blaye, Bordeaux *supérieur*, Bourg, Entre-deux-Mers (light, medium sweet), Graves (medium dry and dry), Loupiac, Côtes de Bordeaux (medium dry), St Foy, and Sauternes. The last-named produces the finest of all French sweet wines, the delectable Château d'Yquem. It may be relevant to note here that in wine the word *supérieur* has no necessarily qualitative connotation, only geographical: it simply means a location, say, upriver, as opposed to *inférieur*, not indicating inferior but 'lower down'. The same with *haut*, meaning 'high'; that is, higher on a slope, more northerly, upstream. It should not be read as indicating higher quality, but it may be coincident with it: Haut-Médoc happens to contain the finest Médoc vineyards. The opposite is *bas* (low), eg Bas-Rhin (Lower Rhine), home of some fine Alsatian wine.

Burgundy red

The basic controlled place names of the Burgundy district are, from north to south, Chablis, Côte d'Or (sub-divided into Côte de Nuits and Côtes de Beaune), Chalonnais, Mâconnais, and Beaujolais. There are over 60 sub-divisions in Côte d'Or alone. Gevrey-Chambertin – to give a name beloved of red Burgundy-lovers – is itself sub-divided nine times.

In red Burgundies (Côte d'Or), here are the great names which, with one exception, I give without variable prefixes, suffixes or sub-divisions: Corton, Beaune, Musigny, Montrachet, Fixin, Chambertin, Nuits-St Georges, Santenay, Côte de Nuits, Volnay, and Vosne-Romanée (Echezeaux, La Tache, Richebourg, Romanée-St Vivant, Romanée-Conti, La Romanée). From the Chalonnais, Mercurey is the only wine you are likely to encounter widely; from the Mâconnais, it will probably be Mâcon supérieur.

Sub-divisions of Beaujolais probably most widely known are B-Villages, B-Supérieur, Brouilly, Chénas, Fleurie, Juliénas, Morgon, Moulin-à-Vent, and St Amour. Pendants tend to exclude Mâcon and Beaujolais from any Burgundy list; French legal classification is on my side.

Only a small proportion of Burgundies, the finest, are estate (*domaine*) bottled. Many of the most notable are dignified by the definite article, ie La Tache, La Romanée. These enjoy special reputation and attract a high price. Red Burgundies, other than Beaujolais, have a more robust character than Bordeaux, but are just as smooth. The largest quantity is simply known as Bourgogne, or Bourgogne *ordinaire*. For my money they are better than the Bordeaux *ordinaries*. To obtain a sound red Burgundy, observe the rules I suggested for Bordeaux, with obvious changes of detail: for example, words like 'ler *Cru*' may be found on red Burgundy bottles but they rarely have any real meaning.

Burgundy white

There is an overlapping of names. For example, under Montrachet, Chassange-Montrachet is a notable red, but there is also a white one, and le Montrachet and the famous Bâtard-Montrachet, are wholly white; celebrated Puligny-Montrachet is mainly white. Some other notable names in white Burgundies are: (Côte d'Or) – Corton-Charlemagne, Meursault, St Aubin; (Chablis) – Chablis, Petit Chablis, Chablis ler Cru; (Mâconnais) – Mâcon *blanc*, Macon Villages, Pouilly-Fuissé; (Beaujolais) – Beaujolais *blanc*; (Chalonnais) – Mercurey, Rully. White Burgundies are all dry. There is a considerable amount of simple Bourgogne *blanc* and a lighter Bourgogne *aligoté*, a pleasant wine of which some is turned into excellent white sparkling wine. Sparkling red Burgundy (Bourgogne *mousseux*) is not much considered in Britain though mildly popular in the USA.

Grapes coming into the *chais* at Pichon-Lalande.

Top left Grapes arriving at the *chais* at the Château Loudenne, and *top right,* a de-stalking machine at the same château.

Above left A Burgundy cellar, and *above right,* old bottles of Beaune stored in a cellar in the Burgundy district.

Rhône

The Côtes du Rhône are a viniferous continuation south from Burgundy, associated with particularly robust red wine, but also producing considerable amounts of white. As they seem to carry less prestige than run-of-the-mill Burgundies, they may offer improved value. The most famous red is, of course, Châteauneuf-du-Pape. Other names to conjure with are Côte Rôtie, Cornas, Hermitage (and Crozes-Hermitage), St Joseph. A rare white is Condrieu, others of importance being St Péray, and both Hermitages. Perhaps the best and most potent French rosé, Tavel, comes from this area, and Lirac is another excellent white or rosé wine.

Loire

Moving north-west from the top of the Burgundy country we come to the Loire, productive of some most attractive white wine, largely of a light and fresh style. The best known wines of the region come from their own districts: Anjou, for rosé d'Anjou, Saumur and Côteaux de la Loire, not to be confused with smaller Côteaux du Loir (a tributary river); Muscadet; Pouilly-sur-Loire, for Pouilly Fumé, an excellent dry white rivalling the better-known Burgundian Pouilly Fuissé; Touraine for Bourgeuil, Chinon and the celebrated Vouvray. The latter is often sold in *pétillant* form. In the Sancerre district one will often find Appellation Contrôlée Sancerre wine, a delectable white, surprisingly expensive. Order a Sauvignon – called for the grape and therefore not name controlled – and you will have a comparable wine for much less. Loire wines have a reputation for 'not travelling': this is nonsense, but they are mainly delicate, should be locally bottled, and are not designed for very long keeping.

Alsace

In this large Rhineland wine-growing district of France, legal control is by grape types and not by location of vineyards: you are most likely to see Traminer (and slightly more prestigious gewürtz-traminer), Sylvaner or Riesling on bottles of Alsatian wines. Thus brand-owners and/or shippers play an important part in assuring you as to the quality of the wines. The town whence the wine comes may also be valid: Colmar, Riquewihr, Bergheim and Guebwiller are notable. You may come across Tokay d'Alsace. This has nothing to do with Hungary but is a local name for the *Pinot gris* grape. Alsatian wines have affinity to some hocks, but never come within spitting distance of the quality of the average of those. They are pleasant medium-dry lightish wines for the most part, and not too costly.

Numerous other parts of France produce table wines of varying standard, but of little consequence.

Champagne

Deliberately I have left this with which to conclude my round-up of France.

View of the fields and grounds of the Samgora Vine Growing State Farm, Georgia, USSR.

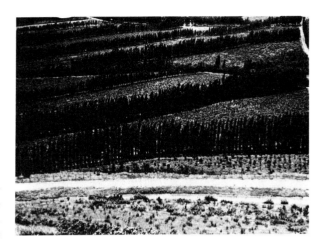

It appears that Louis XV originated Champagne as we know it by allowing it to be bottled for his household, whereas it had previously been a well-known still wine. That may be. I know I prefer the story of its origin through the semi-mythical, blind Dom Perignon, cellarer to the Abbé of Hautevilliers. Dom Perignon is credited with inventing the secondary fermentation in bottle to produce an effervescent wine, and presumably, an embryonic process of *dégorgement* (see below) without which the wine would have been fizzy enough but unpleasantly clouded with sediment.

Perhaps more visitors go to Champagne than to any other place to witness the production of wines, but I will outline the *méthode champénoise*. The wine, from black and white grapes, or both, is carefully blended, and rested in large vats, or in casks for superior grades. The spring following the vintage, it is bottled and fitted with a temporary closure. The bottles are placed neck downwards in racks stretching for miles in deep cellars, and are constantly turned – the *rémuage*. This shakes any sediment that falls down into the neck. At the same time, the secondary fermentation that has taken place charges the wine with carbon dioxide. The fermentation only lasts a few months but *rémuage* continues for years. Then the neck of the bottle is frozen, the temporary cap is removed, and the gas forces out a solid lump of sediment. A small amount of wine may be used to top up, and a little grape brandy. A tiny quantity of sugar is added, even for very dry wines, more for sweeter ones. This is the *dosage*, a process, as with the *rémuage*, credited to the great Veuve Clicquot-Ponsardin. The final cork is then wired on. String used to be employed but rats often ate it and the corks popped out. In final bottle, the wine goes on improving, and some connoisseurs prefer the older vintage wines that have lost some of their pristine exuberance.

Right From left to right: a white wine from Meursault in the Burgundy district; a claret from the Château Gruaud-Larose in the St Julien commune, in a slightly longer-necked version of the usual claret bottle; the famous red Burgundy from the Côtes du Rhone, Châteauneuf-du-Pape; a Sauternes, usually sold in plain, clear bottles.
Below Wines from France. From left to right: a white Mâcon, in the traditional Burgundy bottle; the well-known Rosé d'Anjou, in the slightly tapering Loire bottle; white wine from Alsace, called Sylvaner after the grape, and sold in a 'flute' bottle, slightly longer than the hock bottle; Champagne in its thick, solid bottle; and a claret from St Estèphe in the Bordeaux region.

Left A selection of the white wines for which Germany is famous. From left to right: a wine from the town of Nierstein, famed for its vineyards; a Franconian white wine in the traditional German flagon (a similar bottle is used in Portugal, and has been adopted in Australia for the Burgundy-type wine from Victoria); the renowned Liebfraumilch; and a Riesling from the Mosel's biggest wine commune, Zetlingen.
Below Some wines from Italy. From left to right: Barbera from Piedmont; a quality red chianti (Bordeaux-style bottles are sometimes used for the best chiantis); a Ruffino chianti, named from the district north-east of Florence, and sold in the traditional Italian *fiasco;* and an Orvieto, a fruity and slightly sweet wine.

Below Aspects of Champagne corking at Pierry in France.

FASTENING THE CORK WITH WIRE.

PUTTING ON THE TINFOIL.

WRAPPING THE BOTTLE IN PAPER.

The candling process in the Champagne cellar of a California winery. Holding the bottle before the flame of a candle, the winemaker looks at the Champagne to test its clarity.

A vintage is by no means declared every year. In any event, the majority of Champagne sold is non-vintage and not necessarily any the worse for that. Here we have a further example of the importance of the brand-owner as a guarantee of excellence. A non-vintage champagne from one of the renowned firms will be better than a vintage one from any old cellar. Not more than twenty houses make three-quarters of all Champagne. The numbers of actual brands is almost uncountable, despite the rigorous application of Appellation Contrôlée. Quite a lot of frankly rather awful sweet Champagne is sold to the French. Most Champagne for Britain is extra dry, known as *brut,* a word sometimes emphasised as *brut de brut. Blanc de blanc* means the wine is wholly from white grapes, and is considered better for highest quality champagnes, but this is not proven. Champagne *rosé* (pink Champagne) is no longer fashionable. It is usually made by adding red wine during blending, and is a mutation enjoying little esteem in the industry. Cheap Champagne may be made by certain short-cut methods. It is best to pay a little more for an infinitely superior wine. Non-sparkling Champagne wine (Champagne *nature*) is hard to come by as it is more valuable after processing, but it is delightful. Under French law Champagne in itself is sufficient and additional topographical information need not be given: both cork and label must carry the word. The word is totally protected under British law, too, and cannot be qualified: that is, one could not market a 'Cyprus Champagne' as one may a Cyprus sherry. Many countries do not accept this: witness New York State Champagne. (Champagne-style wines I deal with separately under Other Wines, and I do the same regarding opening, drinking, storing.)

Champagnes, even from the great houses, differ markedly: they have a house style which they take great effort to maintain. It is for the drinker to find the brand that best suits his taste and pocket. But please don't buy Champagne if you don't really care for it: it's getting into short supply.

A view of the Bollinger Champagne cellars.

Checking and crating bottles of 'Champagne style wine' in Argentina.

Germany

To the average drinker German wine means one thing: hock. Pedantically, this term, originated by the English, applies to wines from the Rheingau area of the German Rhineland; in practice it describes all white wines from Germany. Not having any protection, hock is also used to describe some lesser white wines from other countries, and this is disliked by the German wine trade which, by tradition and complex laws, maintains remarkably high standards. The word derives almost certainly from Hockheim, whose wines–presumably under her German-born Consort's influence–were said to be a favourite of Queen Victoria. (Hock is also an old English word for a special beer associated with harvest-time.)

Whilst West Germany produces some red wine, it plays no part in her export trade. It is white wines all the way, and in these Germany is, by general consensus, outstanding. At the ultimate top of the vinous scale, for wines too rare and costly to be considered for drinking at meals but to be savoured on their own, the great Sauternes alone can be classed with the supreme hocks. Only a handful of people will drink these in a lifetime of imbibing, so let us return to commonsense.

Under the strict German laws, wine names are founded on localities; ie the well-known Niersteiner comes from Nierstein. Brand-names are not usually used with places of origin. They are, however, employed in conjunction with such a term as Liebfraumilch, which is not topographical. To some extent this has become synonymous with hock. It is said to come from the Liebfrauenkirche, a church in Worms to which is attached a vineyard. When, as is often the case, the word is associated with a reputable firm, it indicates a sound white Rhineland wine, medium-sweet and with plenty of character.

German wine may also indicate the grapes from which it is made. These are most likely to be the same as for Alsatian wines (see above). Those three grape varieties are widely used throughout the world for hock-style wines. The main German districts from the general drinker's viewpoint are Mosel (Moselle), producer of distinctively light and delicate wines owing much to their growth on soil largely composed of slate–Bernkasteler (suffixed Doktor or Graben for great wines) and Piesporter (Goldtröpfchen) excel; Nahe; Rheinhessen, full of bouquet; Rheingau, the senior district producing the finest Hocks; and the Palatinate, for some excellent sweet wines.

Whilst German-bottled wines will tend to be superior, there are some excellent bottlings by British firms. For general purposes, the rule about knowing your shipper, German or British, applies, and there are some famous blended brand-name wines that are wholly reliable. Some indications of special grades are: *kabinett* (cabinet)–specially reserved; *schlossabzug*–estate bottled; *spätlese*–late picked, producing a heavier, probably sweeter, wine; *auslese*–selected (bunches); *beerenauslese*–selected individual grapes; *trockenbeerenauslese*–very late individually selected grapes, shrivelled in the vine, producing the finest of all hocks. Occasionally the grapes are allowed to remain on the vine until frozen by frost, and this is turned into the fabulous ultra-sweet Eiswein (Ice Wine) which, long matured, is very rare and something of an oddity, though the price is no joke. *Originalwein*, and a host of other terms, tell the initiated the wine is wholly natural, unsugared and unblended. A *Fass* (Rheinland) or *Fuder* (Mosel) number indicates the cask from which a wine was bottled, and is sometimes used for fine wines, since German vintners often do not blend a single vintage but make a wine in its individual cask and bottle directly from it. German wines other than from the Rhineland are not widely exported.

There are numerous further tongue-twisting German wine terms. A full comprehension of German wine lore, and law, possibly requires more erudition than for any other country.

An 18th-century German wine press in the Rüdesheim wine museum.

The celebrated
Liebfrauenkirche, near
Worms, which gave its name
to 'Liebfraumilch'.

Above Wine barrels in Germany delightfully
carved and decorated in traditional style.

'There are five reasons for drinking;
the visit of a friend, present thirst, future
thirst, the goodness of the wine, or
any other reason'.
attributed to Père Sirmond, 16th century.

Below German wine tasting ceremony,
Oberwesel.

A Champagne cellar at Rheims, France. In these deep cellars (caves), the bottles are placed neck downwards in racks, and are constantly turned, a process which shakes any sediment that forms into the neck.

Italy

Italy, as the world's largest wine producer, naturally makes a huge variety. None of it is absolutely top quality–some of it is ghastly–but she does send abroad a large quantity of sound table wines that are comparatively inexpensive and excellent to quaff with food, without getting excited about them. (As with other countries, I am initially dealing with table or beverage wines; specialised wines like vermouth, and fortified wines, are separately treated later).

Virtually the whole country produces wine of some type. Abroad, the best known reds are:
Bardolino, light and smoother than some, from around Verona; Barola, possibly the best, a robust Piedmontese wine; Barbaresco not unlike Barola but perhaps more powerful; Chianti, the celebrated robust Tuscan wine, at its best and treated with no reverence admirable for aiding the digestion of pasta, but the word can also cover vinous disasters; Valpolicella, dry, light and perhaps the most generally useful Italian red wine.

Above Range of Italian wines.

Top Tasting and inspection of wines in the Ruffino Chianti cellars at Pontassieve, Italy.

A woman making a wicker flask at Zano, in the
heart of the Chianti Classico area.

Some better-known exported whites are:
Soave, dry without acidity, delicate, and arguably
the best all-purpose white, suave is indeed the word
for it; Frascati, dry white; Orvieto, fruity and
traditionally on the sweet side (*abboccato*) but now
being made in a drier style as well; Verdicchio, akin
to Orvieto but somewhat lighter.

As the name implies, Castelli Romani is grown
near Rome; it it the popular general wine there.
Lacrima Christi (Christ's Tears) owes much to its
Neapolitan name; customarily white, it lacks other
distinction. Est! Est! Est! is a sweetish wine from
the same district, Latium, as Castelli Romani. It is
a sweetish white from Montefiascone, and a digres-
sion as to the peculiar name seems in order. The
story is that a 12th century German bishop, journey-
ing to Rome, sent ahead a servitor with orders to
taste the wine in projected stop-overs. The arrange-
ment was that the scout would mark tavern doors'
Est – 'it is (good)', or *Non Est* – 'it's not'. Coming to
Montefiascone, he found the wine so good he
scrawled *Est* three times. On arrival, the episcopal
connoisseur agreed, and master and man stayed and
drank their way into legend.

Opposite top The Rhine valley is indubitably the most picturesque major wine district of the world. This view is at Assmannshausen; unusually, the grapes are red.
Opposite below Vines trained very high in a vineyard near Rufina (Florence area) from which chianti will be produced.
Above A noble claret comes from this vineyard pertaining to Château Ausonne.
Right At harvest-time, workers wend their way to and from the distant presses on the Manquehue vineyards near Santiago de Chile. Chile is a huge wine producer: her reds are outstanding amongst sound table wines.

Spain

The Spanish wine industry was until recently poorly organised, nor was there any serious control on naming wines for different districts. This is gradually being put right, a fact to be welcomed, since Spain produces excellent wines and perhaps will produce better still when there is less blending of wines from different districts, and when the endeavour to give a spurious 'Burgundy' or 'Sauternes' image, to wines quite capable of standing on their own merits, ends.

I hope in time to see well matured *Rioja* red wines competing with those of Bordeaux which, except at the highest level, they can do on quality and certainly on price. The ordinary wine of Spain, *vino corriente,* is, particularly the red, superior to its equivalents in France or Italy. The *Rioja* whites possibly have less distinction than the reds. The soundest other Spanish wine is *Valdepeñas,* which we know in Britain principally as a strong red wine but which is also a good dry white.

Anonymously, Spanish wine lends to many blended brand-name wines virtues they might otherwise lack.

Above A drawing by Gustave Doré showing a Spaniard drinking in the traditional manner from a *poron.*
Top right A scene in a Spanish restaurant.
Right A Yugoslavian fisherman drinking 'vino'.

Portugal

The best red is Dão, but one does not find it much abroad. Portuguese table wines owe their recent immense commerical success to successful exploitation of Vinho Verde, literally 'green wine', but actually meaning fresh and young, widely grown by small-holders for the main part and blended by large shippers. Low on alcohol, light, and usually mildly effervescent, it seems to conform to modern taste in some social areas. Portuguese *rosé* is arguably the single most popular wine in Britain.

The Mateus villa in Portugal, famous for its wines, especially the well-known Mateus Rosé.

Right The wine cooking process.

Below A press of immense antiquity in use at Funchal, Madeira. Such sights are depressingly rarer as mechanisation invades the world of wine. Madeira wines are marked by several peculiarities: the vines from which they are made are grown in rich volcanic soil, and heat plays an important role in their production. These fortified wines are the most robust and long lived of all wines.

Opposite, top A scene at Orlando Gramp's winery in the Barossa valley, Australia. Australian wines are gaining esteem, though high transport costs make large-scale exporting difficult.

Opposite, bottom A culinary still life with glasses of inviting cold white wine.

Some other wines

Britain brings table wine from most parts of the world. South Africa contributes very sound whites. Australian reds might do better if distance did not harass them with transport costs. Yugoslavia, in Lutomer Riesling (hock), has a wine strongly competing with the Portuguese in bulk. Even the USA, from her immense Californian wine industry, is sending wine hopefully Europewards. Usually known by grape type, plus brand or house name, some of the US 'clarets' in particular have gained professional approval, but price is not very attractive. Hungarian wine has long been esteemed; legendary Tokay is still made, but that in normal commerce is just a sound and robust sweet wine (a dry is also made).

Top and centre Three views of vineyards in California in the 1870s.
Above This abandoned vineyard represents a tragic stage in the history of the California grape trade, when grape surpluses ruined thousands of wine-growers.

But you will have to search, and pay, for a Tokaji Aszu. It should have a label indicating the number of *puttonys*, referring to the number of buckets (*puttonys*) of over-ripe hand-picked grapes which have been added to the original wine; the higher the number the richer the eventual wine. Enough of exoticism. The Hungarians produce a more mundane but excellent red wine, known as Bull's Blood.

Some interest is being shown in English wine and there has been talk of putting more capital into it. By English wine, I do not mean the various British wines—tonic or desert—which are made from imported juice or concentrates, nor home-made wines, nor the excellent 'country wines' (elderberry, cowslip and the like) produced commercially. I refer to wine proper. There used to be a considerable English wine output, for there is nothing climatically to inhibit satisfactory vine growth and grape ripening in southern England; similar conditions pertain in many European wine-growing areas. From the dissolution of the monastries onward, English wine-making descended into oblivion. Vineyards have

now been re-established successfully as far north as Lincolnshire, and there are others in Surrey, Sussex, Pembrokeshire, Carmarthenshire, Hampshire (commercially viable for years), and the Isle of Wight (the largest is 10 acres). The wine produced is a white Mosel style for the most part, and of excellent quality. What does hold up serious extension is the fact that vines must be at least three years old before bearing a real crop and there is a further maturing period before an investor can hope for any return.

A huge amount of wine imported never sees the bottle on its own. It is for blending. This has resulted in giving a public to whom wine-drinking is a novelty a chance to obtain sound wines—carrying only a brand-name and the country or countries of origin, without further indications of type—and to discover whether they like certain basic types: sweet, dry, white, red, rosé, pétillant, sparkling, strong, thin, pungent, delicate . . . then they can move on to a gradually more detailed appreciation and understanding. Get to know the simple blended brand-name wines; don't despise them. But don't think them more than they are.

Keystone Burgundy

We are the proprietors of Hall's Wine, and have an unquestionable reputation for medicated wines.

Keystone Burgundy is not medicated, but a natural wine solely controlled by us; and it is not particularly for invalids. It is not to battle with illness, but to combat the wear and tear of every-day life; to supply the system with a maximum of nourishment and natural stimulant at a minimum cost.

For the same reason, and on same occasions, as you drink beer, stout, burgundy, or claret, you should drink Keystone Burgundy.

The questions of whether it is better and cheaper you can decide for yourself at our risk. We will send one bottle or twelve bottles, and if you do not like Keystone Burgundy you may send it back, and we will refund your money in full.

Keystone Burgundy is ferruginous; that is, it contains iron naturally, which it acquires by the grapes being grown on soil with iron and limestone in it.

It is a pure, natural wine. Delicious in flavour; not the least inky, although it has iron in it; and it is free from acidity.

**18/- per dozen bottles, carriage paid.
Single bottle, 1/6.**

Stephen Smith & Co., Limited, Bow, London, E.

No. 23.

Above An advertisement for British burgundy.
Above left Gilbey's wine store in Tichfield Street, London.
Top A beautiful and unusual setting for a wine tasting room is provided by this fine display of antiques in a California winery.

Right Many a visitor comes to grief trying to use a *venecia*. Here we see an expert taking a sample of Dry Sack from a cask in Jerez and pouring it into a traditional *copita* without spilling a drop.
Below Preparing for a sherry sampling in cellars at Jerez.
Opposite top left The finished product is bottled and sealed.
Opposite top right Cask making is still very much a handicraft in the sherry business in Spain.
Opposite bottom Sweeping' grapes for pressing in the Algarve, Portugal.

Top left Beside the Lake of Geneva, the Lavaux vineyard rests under Swiss snow until, come summer, Swiss sunshine will ripen the grapes which will make fine Swiss wine.

Top right Grapes being tipped into old collecting vats, Sitten, Switzerland.
Above Vineyard below towering Valeria castle Sion (Valais), Switzerland.

Top left Protection against frost for newly-planted vines in Switzerland.
Top right Manpower still has its place in the technology-orientated wine industry.

Above Collecting tubs of traditional design prior to the grape harvest at Auvernier, Lake Neuchatel, Switzerland.

Above The four basic types of sherry, ranging from dry to sweeter and heavier cream sherry. Those shown are, from left to right *fino, oloroso, amontillado* and cream sherry.

Top A portwine boat leaving Oporto with its cargo.

Sparkling wines

Other than unique Champagne, there are a great many sparkling white wines. These enjoy enormous popularity both in their countries of origin and overseas. What I consider the premier Italian sparkling wine is exported exclusively to the USA, where it enjoys an enormous reputation with Italian-Americans: it is as costly as fine Champagne. Italian sparkling wines are known as *spumante,* and the principal centre for their production is in or around Asti so that Asti-spumante is the most likely description, and sometimes simply the town's name is used to mean a sparkling Italian wine.

In France the generic term is *vin mousseux.* The French also produce artificially carbonated wines (*gazeifié*) which I have not found in export and are best avoided in France. Technically Champagne is a vin mousseux, but never carries that description.

The German version is called *sekt.* There is a very high quality form carrying the prefix *Pradikats.*

Spanish sparkling wine is not to be despised, particularly when one is in Spain, but I would not put it in the same class as the better sparkling wines from France, Germany and Italy. Sparkling wines are made in all wine countries but almost wholly for local consumption: Russians adore their Crimean 'champagne'.

Top quality vin mousseux, spumante or sekt are made by the Champagne method. Comparable results can be–but are not always–achieved by the less expensive *cuve close* method. In this, the secondary fermentation that makes the natural effervescence does not take place in bottle but in pressure tanks.

Spumante is usually medium-dry. Both sekt and vin mousseux come in medium-dry and very dry (*brut*) style. At their best, these wines are superior to indifferent Champagne–and that does exist. They have no pretensions to rivalling quality Champagne, and they are not a substitute for it. They deserve appreciation in their own right.

Luigi Catto wine shop in Elba.

Below Interior of a wine 'supermarket' in Massachusetts.

Top right and above Two views of a wine festival in Vevey, Switzerland.

Fortified wines

These are so called because at a stage in their production they have grape alcohol added to them. Originally this was probably done to give longevity: it became an inherent characteristic of the wines.

Sherry

The name derives from Jerez (the Moorish 'Scheriz') and an earlier form was Sherris Sack. Sack was once employed to describe several wines imported into England, not just that from Jerez. Jerez de la Frontera is the centre of the enormous sherry trade. It lies on the torrid Andalusian plains, surrounded by arid fields where the vines send down deep roots and produce abundant grapes, all white. In September, they are picked and laid to dry on grass mats in order to concentrate the sugar content. Some pressing is done by human feet, encased in spiked boots so that the pips are not unduly crushed – which would produce too much acrid tannin – but this is mainly for the benefit of visitors. Most pressing is mechanical. Fermentation is immediate and violent, and continues for a long time in less tumultuous form, turning all the sugar into alcohol and producing an exceedingly dry wine. For no known reason some of this wine, quite at random, produces a thick growth of *flor,* a type of fungus. It cannot be induced to grow. Such wine will be classified as *fino;* otherwise it will be known as *oloroso.* Both are dry. The only naturally sweet sherry is PX (from the Pedro Ximenez grape), specially made for blending into the sweeter types. Some of these – though sweet sherry is not necessarily dark – will be coloured with *viño de color,* which isn't really wine at all but a juice concentrate. Viño de color and PX are combined to make Paxarete. This is not only employed in Jerez but is what is used for 'wine treating' casks for maturing Scotch whisky.

The wine is re-casked, tested for quality, and grape brandy added: less for fino than for oloroso. The wine then goes into *criaderas* (nurseries) until it earns the right to enter the bodega of the sherry house involved.

In the bodegas, immense and surprisingly cool above-ground cellars, the Solera system is practised. Briefly, this means that as wine is drawn from the oldest cask, it is topped from the next senior cask, and so on up the scale. Only a little wine is taken from each final cask for blending into the shipment sherry to be sent out: there are thousands of casks in a bodega. In effect this means a constant maturing of a wine of identical type, the younger wines benefiting from contact with the older. It is a peculiarity of sherry blending that a very little of the finest and oldest will work miracles on a less mature wine. A cask may have lain nigh on a century, topped up at intervals, giving immense authority to the final blend. Constancy and quality are the keynotes of sherry production. Though such a thing

Top An old print showing the traditional method of pressing the sherry grapes in Jerez.
Above Baskets of grapes for *fino* sherry picked and waiting for collection.

exists, in commerce vintage sherry is unknown.

In commerce, the types of sherry encountered are: Fino–dry, or extremely dry; Oloroso–sweeter, heavier, and usually darker than Fino; Amontillado –a popular compromise style, a type of fino but less dry and with more decided character; the name paying a compliment to Montilla (see below); Manzanilla–very light and dry and, I think, the finest aperitif Fino, matured in bodegas by the sea at Sanlucar de Barrameda. Cream sherry is well sweetened Oloroso: Bristol Cream is a registered trade mark. Bristol Milk is made by many companies and is a title of great antiquity. There are many fine cream sherries from celebrated houses. Brown sherry, sometimes called 'Amoros', lacks its former popularity: it is heavily coloured, sweetened Oloroso. Brand and house names play an important part in quality recognition. Flavours in a sherry style vary considerably from brand to brand.

Sherry is made from California to New Zealand. In Britain, the word on its own may only be applied to the Spanish product. If it be Cyprus cream sherry, of which several brands sell outstandingly well, the country of origin must be as clearly stated as the magic word sherry. The same with any other similar wines, such as South African sherry, which I think is the best non-Spanish wine in the 'dry' area.

Very similar to sherry is **Montilla,** but it may not so be called. Montilla is produced in or around Cordoba. The district both brings in wine to turn into Montilla and sends wine to Jerez to become sherry. Basically production of Montilla is similar to that for sherry, but instead of casks, huge ceramic jars, *tianajas,* with timber covers, are employed. They are not unlike giant Greek amphorae. The very dry Montillas are extremely attractive, deserve to be better known, and are not expensive.

Above Port awaiting shipment.
Top left Jerez, Spain: casks of sherry awaiting shipment, and, *Top right* being loaded on board ship.

Above A sherry seller in Arcos de la Frontera, during a fiesta. The Spaniards were not always great drinkers of sherry, regarding it as an English taste, but it is now gaining popularity.

An 18th-century view of Oporto, Portugal, the centre of the portwine industry.

Port

Port-style wines abound, South African being pre-eminent, but none pretend to rival the port of Portugal. Port is drunk in different forms in numerous countries (as *porto* in France), but its popularity owes much to Britain. The Methuen—better known as the Port Wine—Treaty of 1703, still in force, gave special place in the British market to Portuguese wines. The British took to port in a remarkable way and invented **vintage port,** which is relished only by them and a scattering of Americans.

Alternately drenched and baked, the vineyards (*quintas*) of the Douro are prolific, but the Portuguese government only allows a percentage of the crop to become port, to preserve quality and maintain its value. Much becomes simple table wine or is distilled. The skins are left with the juice during fermenting to obtain as much colour as possible. Fermentation is speedy and the wine is soon vatted, and grape brandy, of which the quality is important, is added. This stops further fermentation, and the wine thus retains a lot of sugar. After some months, the vats are emptied into casks and the wine transported to Vila Nova de Gaia, across the river from Oporto, where it is stored in *adegas,* not unlike the Spanish *bodegas,* known in English—and the British influence is heavy in the industry—as lodges. The headquarters of the trade, the Factory House, or, to be pedantic, the British Association, is in Oporto. From this wonderful old building, the portwine trade is regulated.

Not long ago, the Portuguese re-defined *vintage port,* admitting a new category, *late bottled vintage.* Original *vintage port* is a wine from a single harvest bottled not more than three years later and matured in bottle. *Late bottled vintage port* is a wine from a single harvest bottled in Oporto after 1 July of the fourth year after the harvest and before 31 December of the sixth year. It is for the shipper to decide to 'declare a vintage'; in exceptional years all shippers

will agree. Wines of the vintage year will be separated from others in his lodge and not blended with those of any other year. Vintage (not late bottled) port is sent to England after about two years and there bottled and laid down. It will probably be sold, and may remain in the shipper's cellar or be transferred to the purchaser's. But it will not be ready for drinking for a long time, say twenty years. It will continue to mature virtually indefinitely, though it may require re-corking. It will probably be stored in bond (Customs-controlled duty-free store) to avoid paying the tax until it is released, the dues being amply covered by the steady appreciation in value of the wine. Vintage ports in the prime of life, from great houses in notable vintage years, are fetching such prices that it appears they are being bought more for investment than for drinking. Surely, one day some Crœsus must pull the cork, or all the intervening decades will have been wasted. Vintage port throws a great deal of sediment (crust), for it improves little in cask—fortified wine improves in wood, but very slowly—and all the real maturing is in the bottle.

Late bottled vintage port has improved longer in wood, requires less bottle life, and throws much less crust. Wines of similar quality, but not bottled under the lb vintage rule, may only be described as late bottled, not as vintage port. Lb and lb vintage are ready in about ten years. They are sold ready for drinking and are within the reach of many.

Another high quality old port is called **crusted port.** This is a blend of fine wines treated in the same way as vintage; thus it throws a big crust and gets its name. The other descriptions of port, and the most likely to be purchased for the average home, are **ruby**—the commonest, about four years in wood; and **tawny**—longer matured in cask and superior blends to ruby. **White port** is simply ordinary port made from white grapes. It is more drunk as an aperitif, chilled, than as a dessert wine.

Top left The fine old building of the Port Wine Institute in Oporto.
Top right Emptying the 'must' from the *borracheiros* in the shippers' lodge.

Above Sending out wine from the stores of the Cadiz, Oporto and Light Wine Association for Christmas consumption.

Madeira

Once as popular as port or sherry, ever since the phylloxera (see Glossary) ravaged the island, Madeira wine has lost way. It deserves revival. The wine, grown on surprisingly rich soil, is extremely robust. It is sometimes called a 'cooked' wine, for a peculiarity of Madeira is that it is matured, for a time, in casks that are subjected to heat, which it is most wine-producers' desire to avoid. Superior Malmsey, the famous rich, dark, dessert Madeira, is rested in the sun. The other three types are subjected to treatment in stores called *estufas* (stoves) which are heated well above 100° F. This would kill most wines. They are then fortified with a heavy dose of grape brandy and matured in a Solera-style system as for sherry. Bual is a cheaper form of Malmsey. Verdleho is a medium dry; and Sercial is light and dry. In their respective flavour areas, they are for drinking as with sherry or standard ports.

Two other once famous dessert wines have lost much of their popularity. One is **Malaga,** named for the Spanish town, owing much to the addition of PX (see Sherry) to the local wine, plus grape brandy. The other is **Marsala,** which has an interesting history. John Woodhouse went to Sicily to find his fortune: he did. He discovered a pleasant sweet local white wine. Sending a batch to London, he added alcohol to ensure its preservation. This Marsala became enormously popular, rivalling port, sherry or Madeira, and 'Old John' and his family became fabulously rich. It did no harm when Nelson bought copious supplies for his fleet. From the beginning of this century, the export declined. Marsala is recognised as a wine type under Italian law. It is a blend of wine, concentrated raisin extract, sweet grape juice and burnt sugar which give it a distinctive flavour. With egg and sugar it forms the basis of zabaglione, the well-known Italian dessert.

IMMENSE CASK OF PORT WINE.

THIS huge Cask, or Tonel, of Port Wine, shipped from Oporto by Mr. F. W. Cosens, of No. 4, Hart-street, Mark-lane, has just been landed in the St. Katherine's Docks, from the brig *Pezo da Regoa*, Captain Herbert; and its extraordinary size has excited considerable interest.

It has been long allowed by competent judges, that wine, of all fermented liquors, is the one that develops its high vinous character more fully in a large bulk, like the present, than it is possible for it to do in the casks (little more than one-sixth the size) usually employed for transmission to this country. To prove this, the present monster cask has been sent; and it is, we understand, the importer's intention to adopt this mode in future of transmitting to this country his most *recherché* wines.

Above A humorous 19th-century illustration.
Top Madeira wine being made at a wine lodge in Funchal, Madeira.

Vermouth

This could be described as a fortified wine, but it is more a manufactured one, and I feel comes into a category of its own. It is a worldwide product, but is peculiarly associated with Italy and, to a lesser extent, France. The word describes a type of product and is not in itself protected. Two famous brand-names dominate the industry, but the number of brands made is enormous.

There are legendary origins to vermouth going back to the wine of Hippocrates 2500 years ago, or the wormwood-flavoured wine of the Romans. The virtues of the wormwood flower, which in excess can be poisonous, have long been known, especially in eras when worming potions were valued by people amongst whom intestinal parasites were endemic. For this purpose *wermutwein* (wormwood wine) was employed centuries ago in South Germany. To be slightly more factual, it seems established that a Piedmontese gentleman saw possibilities in this combination of therapeutic herb and wine and took the recipe to Paris in the 16th century, where it enjoyed some success, medicinally, in court circles. The French gallicised the word to *vermout* but did little about exploiting it. Quite a long time later, in 1678, we hear of an Italian savant praising something like vermouth, and a similar product was being made in northern Italy under control of the Turin distillers' guild. That is significant, as Piedmont remains the vermouth centre and Turin its capital. At that time vermouth was a separate compound which people added to wine in desired quantities. (I use the unnecessary 'h' which the English added in due course, one of their erratic contributions to the semantics of the world of drinking). Though a firm now in business existed earlier, 1786 is thought to have seen the introduction of a brand of ready-mixed vermouth. In 1840, Turin vermouth was protected by the issue of royal licenses. Vermouth had left its medicinal past and was embarked on a highly successful social career.

Insufficient wine is made in Piedmont to supply today's giant industry, nor do the hills adjacent to Turin any longer provide the herbs that give vermouth its special flavours. Wine comes from all over Italy, and botanical ingredients from all the continents. Up to fifty may be required for a single formula: books in the Martini museum list as many as 200 required in the past! The basic herbal essence, the secret of the brand, is thoroughly married with highly filtered white wine and the infusion fortified with grape brandy. Sugar is mixed in for sweet red (*rosso*) and the sweeter white (*bianco*) types. After further resting to ensure complete harmony between the ingredients, the vermouth is totally refrigerated, which obviates any likelihood of the wine throwing a deposit on prolonged storage. It is pasteurised and filtered very thoroughly before bottling, which may take place where it is made or overseas.

'French' is the word sometimes used to describe dry or ultra-dry vermouth since that style was developed there. 'Italian' used to be used to describe the traditional sweetish red. Today both styles are made in France and Italy. In fact, vermouth is normally ordered by preferred brand-name with a description of the type wanted. Vermouth will keep indefinitely in bottle. Opened, it keeps well but I suggest that a dry one, in particular, should there only be a little in the bottle, had better be put into a smaller container if it is not for immediate use. It is, of course, one of the great ingredients for mixed drinks, but is agreeable enough on its own, or as a mixture of sweet and dry. I prefer to chill the wine rather than put ice in it: one gets a better flavour. Vermouth is a flavoured wine, and a delightful one.

A separate type of vermouth from France is **Chambéry** from the Savoy department, of which the original dry variety is not quite the same as a 'French'. It is an admirable aperitif, for drinking without gin or vodka fortification, but lightly chilled. There is a very full-flavoured red, and a 'bittered' Americano Chambéry. The most unusual of all is the deliciously different **Chambéryzette** which is tinged with the bouquet of local wild strawberries. Another distinctive vermouth is the bittersweet **Punt e Mes.**

Branded aperitif wines

The best-known is indubitably **Campari.** Its strength of 45 proof (British) qualifies it as a spirit, but it is essentially wine-based. Only three or four people know the formula. One either adores or cannot abide its bittersweet taste. Now an industrial giant, the firm's story started in 1842 when 14-year-old Gaspare Campari arrived in Turin, the vermouth capital, and was apprenticed to a liqueur manufacturer. He took his craft to Milan and there invented the recipe for Campari Bitters which was to make his name world famous. Other **aperitifs** are:

Suze, a gentian-flavoured wine aperitif.

Byrrh, best called 'aperitif Byrrh' so as to avoid getting beer; it is said, unique amongst aperitifs, to improve in bottle.

Dubonnet, a sweetish French fortified wine with a tangy quinine after-taste. The white (*blonde*) variety is sweeter. An excellent mixer.

St Raphael, a fortified herb-flavoured wine with quinine; red or white.

Lillet, herb and quinine flavoured, and made with wine of unusually high quality; serve very cold with twist of lemon.

Whisky-flavoured wine is dealt with under Spirits (Whisky-based brands).

Opposite One of the well-known Cinzano advertisements.

Taste the bright lights!

This Christmas, try Cinzano Bianco.
It's a unique and subtle taste - light, bright and slightly sweet.
You can serve it on its own with ice and a slice of lemon. Or with soda
for a really refreshing long drink. There's nothing else quite like it.
It's the Bright Lights Taste !

Buying wine

This was once, and, if you are happily situated financially, still can be, the pleasant matter of going to a merchant, talking, sampling and ordering. You will be surprised how many wine merchants there still are who are delighted to see new customers. Your needs do not have to be large. A good wine merchant has this in common with a good bank manager: he is looking ahead. Your order may be modest now, yet when you have 'arrived' who knows but that your business will be really valuable to him? So do not feel abashed at going to even the most prestigious house. If you are tidy, sober and in your right mind, you will be courteously received, even if you only require a bottle of respectable claret because the boss is coming to dinner that evening.

In those sections of the market where speedy turnover of stocks and limitation of number of lines carried are prime considerations–the supermarket arena–it would be unreasonable to expect the manager to give individual attention. Here you must exercise your own product and brand awareness and discretion, relating what are purely price factors to other considerations, notably to your knowledge of the reliability of products on sale. You may not have a very wide selection, but you can examine closely what is for sale–and also make comparisons with rival establishments. Where there is keen competition, the wise customer reaps considerable benefits.

There remain a considerable number of wine stores where, though there is an element of self-selection, the manager and even some of his staff will have equipped themselves with more than such minimal information as that a Cheval Blanc is neither a whisky nor a white wine but an exceptional château in Bordeaux. Do not be afraid to test them: they will either indicate their ignorance or, just as likely, be flattered to have their opinion sought and may possibly indicate some bargain. 'End of bin' is always worth seeking. The term means that the firm does not wish to continue stocking a line or has only a few cases left and cannot get more, and it will be going below list price. A few bottles bought thus – in excess of your immediate requirements–may be the foundation of a personal 'cellar'.

Never miss the opportunity to read a wine list. Many of them are loaded with information, and at worst they provide a price guide which may serve you well in restaurants where wine mark-ups continue in the main to be outrageously high.

If you can afford it, watch out for wine auctions like Sotheby's or Christie's; occasionally wine will come up in other auction-rooms. These are not only for the big spenders. You take a chance with older wines that may have 'gone over the top', but the lots are not necessarily cumbersomely large and this is not only an exciting way of buying wines; it can be very profitable. Old champagnes seem a specially fertile area for bargains because a lot of folk are suspicious of them, usually without any justification whatsoever.

I do not propose to deal with wine as a purely financial investment. However, spare cash put into wine for your own use is money well spent. Prices of sound wine–let alone great wine–can only go up. The earlier you buy, the better; that is to say, if you buy claret before it is ready for drinking, you will get it very much cheaper than when it has matured. If you have not a cellar–and how many people have today?–the merchant from whom you purchase may store it for you, possibly for nothing, but today perhaps making a small charge. Wine ready for use may often also be left with a reputable store or merchant, and you draw off supplies as required.

Keeping wine

However, quite a lot of wine will go into a comparatively small space. Wine is more robust than some would let us think. The main thing is to find a place in the home which is not subject to violent changes of temperature, like the loft, or is too warm, like the airing cupboard; under the stairs is a popular spot, and if it means tossing out an old bicycle and three broken tennis rackets, that's all to the good. Flats provide more problems. Even there, a place can be found in the hall as a rule, but as far from any central heating point as possible. I have entirely satisfactorily kept wine a fair time in racks in my kitchen/diner. After all, the turn round of a home 'cellar' of this description is pretty quick, and I'm not trying to lay down vintage claret.

Keeping the wine when it is opened is perfectly practicable. Sound table wine, if a bottle be half-emptied, will keep in good condition at least for twenty-four hours, even longer if the temperature is moderate. It should be firmly corked. (If you find difficulty in re-corking a bottle, cut a 'V' in the cork with a sharp knife'. If closed with one of those special and inexpensive patent stoppers, Champagne will keep well and bubbly for a surprisingly long period, preferably in the refrigerator. Sherry and port won't keep for ever, as some people who only open the decanter twice a year think. A couple of weeks is ample for a dry sherry; a sweet one will keep longer, and the better the port the longer it will keep, provided not too much air is in contact with it. It's not that fortified wines deteriorate dramatically, even over a longish time, but they will lose their best manners.

Home wine making is a booming industry. On the opposite page we see some of the processes involved.

Above The final stages in making rose-hip wine.
1. Pouring the wine into bottles. 2. The wine is kept covered as long as possible during bottling, and then left loosely corked in the bottle.
3. After a period the corks are pushed home and the bottles are labelled. 4. Here the wine is ready to drink after having been matured for at least a year.

Above Some stages in making pear wine.
1. Cleaning and wiping the fruit. 2, 3. The pears are placed in a pan and simmered gently, with sugar added.
4. During the fermentation period a lock is often employed.

Serving & drinking wine

Red wine

It is generally accepted that red wine is served at 'room temperature' (*chambré*). Ideally, this means that one stands it in the room in which it will be used for some hours before and that this room will have an even temperature. In practice, a dining-room, unless centrally heated, can in winter be a chilly place, quickly heated before occupation. So stand the red wine in a reasonably warm place – but not on a radiator! This should not be the kitchen, because you should take the cork from the wine a couple of hours before serving; wine benefits from 'breathing' and if it has been long in bottle it appreciates this breath of air the more – but the opened wine must not be so located that it attracts culinary odours. A true Beaujolais, alone amongst red wines, is correctly to be served on the cool side, particularly *new* Beaujolais.

A château-bottled or other aged red wine will contain a variable amount of sediment. Make sure it is well rested. Ideally it will be brought from rack in a 'cradle' which was invented for this purpose, and, not, as is often the case today, for serving the wine from. However, that is a satisfactory enough way to pour a wine, though it needs a steady hand and careful judgement as to the point where the sediment shows. Some restaurants pour all red wines from a cradle, giving ordinary wines a cachet to which they should have no pretensions.

Decanting is preferable in the instance of old red wines. Traditionally a candle is placed below the neck of the bottle (I find a torch more satisfactory) and the wine is carefully poured into the decanter until the sediment begins to arrive at the neck; this is easily visible. If the wine is a fairly grand one, it is permissible to attach the cork to the decanter neck – this is the rule in the case of fine port – so guests may satisfy themselves as to the wine, and the bottle itself should be retained as there may be those present who would wish to examine it.

No such attention is demanded by recently bottled or blended brand-name wines. You can put them in a claret jug if you like for decorative purposes.

A stemmed glass of any shape will do, but not excessively large, and a fairly bulbous glass will concentrate the bouquet of a fine wine. Never fill a glass more than two-thirds full.

White and sparkling white wine

Decanting is not required. There is a tendency to over-chill white wines. My rule is: the poorer the wine the colder. Sweet wines can take rather more chilling than dry. Over-chilling simply refrigerates all taste out of the wine. Fine white wines, and particularly vintage Champagne, are probably best at what is called cellar-temperature – but this is a frigid age and some people do like their white and sparkling wines very cold: often they miss a lot by this habit. It is quite sufficient to bring a white wine – or rosé – chilled to the table. Some sort of coaster will be required to catch the moisture condensing from the bottle. An ice-bucket – not to stand on the table – is in order, but I feel this is more a restaurant than a domiciliary convenience.

Ordinary white wines may be served in the same type of glass as reds. It is customary to serve hock in long-stemmed glasses, the idea being to separate warm hands as far as possible from cold wine. Frequently such glasses are coloured. The custom dates from the time when Rhenish wines were rather muddy and coloured glass disguised this visually displeasing aspect. Today they are bright and clear and much better admired through plain glass.

Champagne, and sparkling wines of quality, are best served in a thin, narrow flute glass which conserves the natural effervescence. The saucer glass, long esteemed because it dissipated the bubbles (which are a characteristic of the wine), is now in disrepute and there are few mourners.

Corks

There is a large variety of corkscrews on the market. I find the best is the simple French boxwood reversing screw which brings out the cork with the minimum effort and disturbance. Expert opinion is divided on the modern air-operated devices which force out the cork by atmospheric pressure: they need careful handling; I don't think anyone would use them for rare vintages, but they cannot harm plain wines. Whatever corkscrew is used, it should be fairly long and with close-knit whorls so as to obtain a good purchase. Corks break from time to time or, are too stubborn to move. In the latter case, if practicable, return the bottle to its point of purchase; in the former, you can do little more than get rid of the cork somehow and filter the wine into a decanter through clean muslin to get rid of the bits.

Champagne and sparkling wines should be opened very carefully, without a loud bang. Whilst removing wire, a thumb should be held over the cork in case it is going to release itself. Be careful never to point the bottle at anyone, for a champagne cork may be subjected to considerable pressure and its ejection may turn the cork into a dangerous projectile. The cork should be eased out, the neck quickly wiped and a little wine immediately poured. If very fizzy, only a little should be put into each glass as it may rise and spill over. Some champagne corks remain obdurately stuck. You can usually release them by pushing upwards with the thumbs, but pliers (there are special ones made) may be needed. I have been reduced to cutting off the bulbous top of the cork and removing the rest with a corkscrew: this undignified procedure is best performed out of sight of guests who will then not hear your profanity.

Cork is porous, which is why wine is stored lying down, so that it may remain moist and not shrink, which would admit air and harm the wine eventually.

Sometimes stored bottles will leak at the cork – such a bottle is known as a weeper – and should then immediately be drunk. The wine itself will probably be all right. An occasional poor cork can taint the wine, though this is rare: hence the expression 'corked'. This is the reason for tasting a wine, before general pouring. At home, the host should do this before it comes to table. To do so in front of guests only proves, as I have said elsewhere, that it is not poisoned!

Decanters

Decanters can be attractive objects, antique or modern. They are really for fortified wines and spirits. A claret jug is more suitable for red wines. A decanter is properly dressed with a decanter label. Antique ones are collector's pieces but admirable reproductions are available in plate and silver, and modern ones (some rather vulgar) in everything from brass (not quite the thing) to ceramic. China antique ones can be attractive and less costly than many.

Decanters, when used for heavy wines, especially port, become discoloured at the base. A mixture of vinegar and ammonia is one remedy, vigorously washed out with water afterwards. Another way is to put potato peelings and a little water in the decanter and to let them disintegrate and ferment, washing out the rather nasty mess in due course. Stoppers have an annoying habit of sticking. Friction with a piece of string looped round the neck may do the trick, or gradually warming the neck with hot water so it minutely expands before the stopper. If empty, a little olive oil round the join between stopper and neck, left to penetrate, should release it. Frequently, a cautious bump of the case on a wooden surface is effective – if it doesn't shatter the decanter itself.

As to the question of which wine you serve with which food, there are plenty of pundits to tell you about this. I'm not joining them: mostly their advice is snobbishly archaic. Drink which wine you prefer with what you like. Set your own standards, within the bounds of obvious common-sense, and have the courage of your vinous opinions.

Beer and cider

Beer, since it connotes agriculture, and is not basically a fortuitous product, is probably of more recent origin than wine. Possibly, it's not more than 10,000 years old! Brewing does not necessarily imply beer as we understand it; Japanese *sake* (see below) might as easily qualify as rice-beer as rice-wine, and brews from a great range of materials are made all over the world. It is from a basic beer that such a great product as Scotch whisky comes and junior only to the manager in a whisky distillery is the head brewer. However, for the purposes of this book, the term 'beer' is used to cover the conventional beverages for which the word is colloquially employed. It derives from the continental mainland (*bier, bière,* etc.) and came into the English language with the introduction of hops some 500 years ago. The use of hops improved the keeping qualities of beer, but eventually led to great dissention between the brewers of traditional ale and the newer beer. Distinctions between types of brew gradually waned: we now seem to be moving towards a sort of

Above An 18th-century brewhouse.

international low gravity gaseous fluid of unknown strength. However, some of the old art of the brewer still survives.

Malted barley is the basis of beer. The grain is soaked, allowed to germinate, and dried. It is lightly dried for light beers and roasted dark for dark beers and stout. The malt is then crushed and may be mixed with other unmalted cereals, according to the type of beer, before mashing–that is, infusing into boiling water. The wort (sugar liquid) is drawn off. The process is repeated to obtain all sugar from the mash.

To the wort is added more sugar, and the hops, more or less a quantity according to style, are added and boiled into the liquid, which at this stage is non-alcoholic. The wort is strained to remove the hop residue. Yeast now comes into the picture. This turns the sugar in the wort into alcohol and at the same time produces much carbon dioxide. We now have beer, unclarified and unrefined. It is simple to make beer; what is not so simple is to make it on the gigantic scale required by modern demand. Not

that more beer is drunk than in the past, when it provided whole populations with their sole drinking matter (water being despised on good, if uncomprehended, health grounds). The local brewer, the brewhouse attached to farm and many houses, supplied that demand. A modern brewery uses the most sophisticated techniques, automated and computerised to the nth degree. It is undeniably impressive, though almost inhuman in its complex efficiency. But the customers seem happy enough on the whole. Beers for transport and export, which must travel for thousands of miles in bulk containers could not be made by the old methods. The industry knows no frontiers. American beer is sold in London, Dublin stout in the Far East, Burton brews in Brussels, Belgian lager in London, French beer in Munich, Australian beer in Brighton . . . In bottle, can, and canister, beer flows round the world, but not very often in wooden cask. The internationalisation of beer is a recent and growing aspect of the liquor trade which has interesting social implications.

The splendour of the old English pub is undimmed—even if every year fewer superb ones rest intact. Here we see a typical Victorian exterior (rarely matched by modern commercialism), and, in the same brewery's control, a remarkable example of ebullient yet elegant interior design, rich in fine and irreplaceable woodwork. How many elbows have polished the top of that splendid bar, how many shoulders found welcome support against that great mahogany pillar, how many feet been comforted by that gleaming brass rail—and how many pints spilt on that marble floor?
Traveller! seek these glorious relics of Britain's bibulous past. Britons! cherish such places as remain.

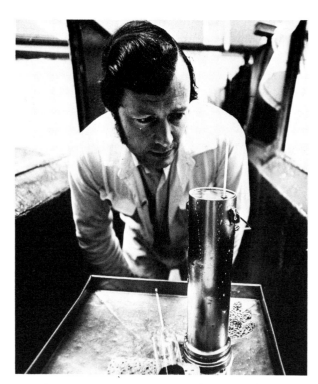

Left Testing at Ind Coope's brewery in Romford. *Below* Bottling at Farsen's brewery in Malta. *Bottom* Bass Charrington's Burton-on-Trent brewery. Bass and Worthington bitter are seen fermenting in casks.

Above View of fermenting vessels at Allied Breweries' establishment at Wrexham.
Top The central control panel at the new brewhouse of Allied Breweries, Burton-on-Trent.
Left The heart of the best British beer—a hop cone, ripe and ready for picking.

Below Hop pickers in Tasmania and *(bottom left)* in Kent. *Bottom right* The hops transported by lorry after picking.

Below A Morris dancer enjoys a pint.
Left and bottom Hops being dried and stored in 'pockets'.

There are enormous variations in strength and quality in the basic types of beer, which can be divided into:

Bitter, an essentially English brew, in its traditional form strongish, heavy, flat, and served at cellar temperature (whatever that might happen to be). Its gravity has generally been decreased and it is lighter, livelier and is often served cool. The average large-scale bitter is a prime example of how beers are tending towards an hygienic anonymous norm. (Prime, small brewery, casked bitter, clarified and conditioned in the pub cellar and drawn from the wood directly or by gravity pump, is increasingly rare and, when found, is to be cherished).

Lager, a term meaning literally beer conditioned by long maturing in a very cold store (lager). There are also differences in mashing and fermentation, which is longer than for beer. Munich was its home town, and much Munich beer is the original dark lager. It is said that the secret of making lager, and a very special yeast, were taken from Munich to Pilsen about a century and a half ago. Pilsen had been a brewing city since time immemorial. With the new yeast they started, too, to make lager, a light-coloured style, now referred to as Pilsener even if not made there. True Pilsener-type lager is made in Germany and Czechoslovakia and is worth the money it costs. The type has been repeated in the hundreds of lagers and lager-type beers, which are the most popular style globally. In a decade the sale of lager in Britain has risen tenfold. Lager, mass produced, is the basis of the internationalism to which I have referred. Even if some of the beers are not technically lager, they have similar taste characteristics. Lager should be drunk cold; the superior qualities are better appreciated if only slightly chilled.

Stout, there are others, but Guinness so dominates this brewing area that it has to be mentioned by name. It is obtainable in virtually every country in the world and is brewed in a number as well as in

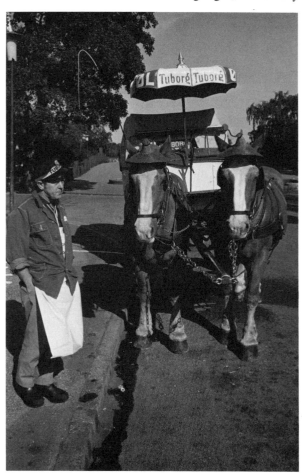

Above Tuborg brewery horses, Copenhagen. Only four of these horses are still working, but the tradition will be kept going as long as possible.
Top right Beer drinking in the Transkei, South Africa.
Right The Ale-wife of England, a ballad by John Skelton.

86

Dublin and London. It is remarkable how popular stout is in tropical Africa. This is as natural a beer as can be produced under industrial conditions.

Mild, a weak, sweet, traditional English beer that is disappearing.

Burton, dark, heavy, strong, and dry, sometimes made in winter by British breweries.

Keg, bitter style, in pressurised kegs. Stout and other styles are also being kegged for handling and serving convenience.

Draught, this only means coming from a container, large or small, and not from a bottle.

Bottled, said to have been discovered by a Dean of St Paul's in 1563, when he left a bottle of ale on an outing. When he re-found it, he discovered the contents had matured and become effervescent. Commercially, beer could not be satisfactorily bottled until the discovery of a satisfactory closure. The best bottled beers are considered to be those matured in bottle, making their own gas—also a sediment which needs careful pouring (though some drinkers relish it 'all in'). Most bottled beers, and all canned, are, like the majority of today's beers, pasteurised, filtered and inert, the gas going in at the time of bottling.

Barley wine, extra strong ale, often sold under proprietary names.

Audit ale, etc, special beers brewed to mark anniversaries, coronations and the like; for collecting rather than drinking nowadays.

Stingo, strong dark ale with a sharp tang; not very common.

Brown ale, self-descriptive; on the sweet side.

Russian stout, extremely strong vintage stout, long matured.

IPA (Indian pale ale, or simply **pale ale**), was originally made for export. Is the basis of a range of beers with proprietary names.

A beer stand in the Soviet Union.

Top 'Peasants in an inn', a painting by the
17th-century Dutch artist, Van Ostade.
Above A 17th-century alehouse.
Opposite A Bavarian couple rather gloomily
partaking of refreshment. They are drinking from
the traditional earthenware mug.
Right 'Modern Midnight Conversation', a
satirical painting by Hogarth. These gentlemen
will doubtless be in need of a hangover cure
(see page 99).

Piles of staves waiting to be made into barrels by coopers in Yugoslavia. Although cooperage is a decreasing art, as the demand is less, such barrels are still used for the storage of alcoholic beverages, cider being no exception.

Cider

**'Hundreds of men were turned into beasts,
Like the guests at Circe's horrible feasts,
By the magic of ale and cider'.**
Miss Kilmansegg Thomas Hood

The humorous libel quoted above at least refers to the magic of cider. The apple was held to have mystical qualities by ancient Celts and an apple god was worshipped. By the time Julius Caesar invaded Britain, cidermaking was prevalent, as it was in the part of Gaul we know as Normandy. Cider or cyder was mentioned in monastic writings of early medieval times, and appeared to refer to any intoxicant. In the 14th century cider's popularity was such that an order was required forbidding its use instead of water at baptismal ceremonies. Thereafter literary references to it grew. Bacon and Shakespeare referred to it. Inevitably Pepys mentions drinking 'a cup of syder' (spelling was not yet bound by rules).

It has ceased to be a cottage industry, though the growing of apples is a widespread farming activity. The apples are for the main part collected centrally for cider-production by modern methods. The washed apples are reduced to a pulp (pomace) and pressed through coarse linen. The juice is pumped into vats where immediate fermentation starts through the action of the natural yeast in the apple skins on the sugar in the apples. Special varieties of cider apples have been cultured, just as grapes have for wine. Additional yeast is sometimes added. The cider is fermented completely to make dry cider. For sweet or medium-sweet it is stopped at an appropriate stage to allow a proportion of sugar to remain. Fizzy bottled cider is made by adding CO_2, except for 'champagne' cider which is produced by fermentation in bottle to make carbon dioxide. There is great variety in the alcoholic strength of various ciders, the strongest sometimes being referred to as 'apple wine' (though whether EEC rules will eventually permit that description is open to doubt).

The pomace residue, when all fermentable liquid has been removed, produces pectin, used in setting jams and so on. The residue is good livestock fodder. Cider mixes admirably (and somewhat lethally) with gin: it is a base for excellent variations on cider cup (qv).

An 18th-century apple press.

APPLE CRUSHER

A few well-known alcoholic beverages fit neatly into no category.

Gin sling

With gin sling a brand reference is essential, though I have thought fit as far as possible to avoid naming names. Pimm's now only make their original No. 1 Cup, having discontinued the other five based on different spirits. Near the Bank of England, on the site known to have been occupied by a tavern in 1499, James Pimm, in his oyster bar, invented in the 1840s the first gin sling. His successors bottled and started to sell this thirty years later. Pimm's is based on the finest London dry gin, compounded to the recipe of James Pimm and known only to a handful of people. Under the ægis of independent chemists, modern bottlings are tested from time to time against the original formula to ensure that it remains unchanged in a changing world. Fizzy lemonade, well chilled – better than ice in the drink – and a garnish of lemon and cucumber rind, or the traditional (summer) herb, borage, if available, are all the additions required. A halfpint tankard is the right container, unless it be a pint. The pub/restaurant custom of dolling the drink up with a mass of fruit and foliage is to be deprecated as superfluous and ostentatious.

Mead

This is an aromatic drink of great antiquity; a form of it is referred to in Babylonian laws of 2000 BC. It is difficult to define, being part distillate, part brew, part wine. Its taste basis is honey, plus other herbs. Many medicinal and aphrodisiac virtues have been attributed to it in the past, and some of its admirers make the same claims today.

Sake

The growing popularity of Japanese restaurants makes mention of this necessary. A 'double brew', it has a strength of about 18 per cent alcohol. It is drunk at around body temperature – though, inevitably, today it is sometimes chilled. It is served in *sakazuki*, small china cups. An acquired taste.

Above The apple harvest and, *right* at a Japanese inn at Futami, a cup of sake is being offered to a geisha girl.

Opposite below An old-fashioned apple crusher on Jersey, the Channel Islands. This has not been used for some decades – cider is no longer made in Jersey. In any case, modern methods, such as this new apple harvester *(opposite right)*, are now in favour. This machine can pick up a ton of apples in five minutes.

Top The fabulous Salle des Abbés, Fécamp, Normandy, home of Benedictine, and *above*, the main distillation hall for the production of this best-selling liqueur.

Liqueurs and cordials

Personally, I make a division between sweet liqueurs and cordials; the latter is American parlance for what Europe knows as liqueurs. I think of cordials as lighter and not usually associated with famous brand-names.

True proprietary liqueurs I consider to be:

Bénédictine, has been made in Fécamp, Normandy, by Bénédictine monks since 1510. It has a Cognac base. It is wonderfully digestive; so are many liqueurs. Each label carries the initials DOM which are incorrectly thought to stand for Dominican Order of Monks. Why Dominican, for goodness sake? They are an abbreviation for *Deo Optimo Maximo,* 'to God, most good, most great', and are a reverent tribute from the Bénédictine order who consider their particular nectar truly a gift of God. 'B & B' is a blend of Bénédictine and cognac and is drier.

Chartreuse, the other great monastic liqueur. Ancient, but not commercialised until rather over a century ago. When the monks were expelled from France at the beginning of this century in a wave of anti-clericism, they went to Spain, and the liqueur is still made in Tarragona. When they returned to their monastery near Grenoble, the monks started again making the liqueur in France. It is true they make it, but they neither market nor drink it. It is handled by an outside company, and the royalties support the monasteries' considerable charitable work. The original formula, containing 150 herbs, is the Elixir Végétal, which is not in wide distribution and has a strength of 136 proof British, or very nearly twice the strength of standard British spirits. But the formula is very similar for Green Chartreuse, which is 96 proof. The yellow is sweeter and is 75 proof.

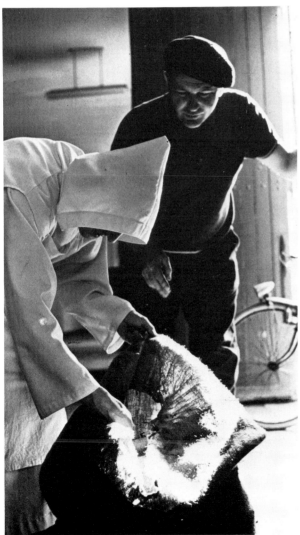

Top The monastery of Chartreuse.
The ingredients of Chartreuse are still a carefully guarded secret, though photographers are allowed to record some of the processes involved in its manufacture.

Left A Carthusian monk holds newly distilled examples of the green and yellow Chartreuse liqueurs for which the monastery (see page 95) is famous throughout the world. *Opposite* A handful of just a few of the multitudinous herbs which go into the highly secret formula. To illustrate, or to mention, all the liqueurs and cordials of the world would need a volume (there is one; by Peter Hailharten) and the illustration *below* is intended simply as a pictorial evocation of this delicious, principally sweet, aspect of the world of drinks and drinking.

Cointreau, this is the finest of orange curaçao, generically known as *triple sec.* The Cointreau family put their name to theirs to avoid confusion with lesser makes. Not only pleasing as a liqueur, it is one of the rare ones that is attractive served 'on the rocks'. It also blends extremely well into a variety of mixed drinks (see Cocktails).

Drambuie, I have already mentioned under Spirits, but no list of liqueurs would be complete without it. The name comes from *an dram buidbeach* (the drink that satisfies). It is based on very fine Scotch, and whilst the palate suggests honey plays a part in the formula, the recipe is very much a secret of the Mackinnon family who claim it was given to them by a grateful Prince Charles, after his 1745 disaster, when they aided his escape from Scotland. (Whether this escape benefited him is open to question: he drank himself to death on brandy.)

Galliano, a superior strega-style yellow Italian liqueur, enjoying particular popularity in the USA. It gained a lot of publicity through the introduction of the Harvey Wallbanger (qv).

Glen Mist, an unusual story lies behind this. When Scotch whisky was very short after World War II, production was transferred to Ireland. It returned to Scotland in 1963, and is now a compound of matured Scotch, herbs, spices and honey: somewhat drier than other whisky-based liqueurs.

Grand Marnier, based on nothing less than *fine champagne* cognac, this has a vague affinity to *curaçao* but is quite distinctive and enjoys a very high reputation.

Goldwasser, a type of Kümmel made in Danzig (Gdansk) from the mid 16th century. When it became fashionable to take gold as a specific for certain diseases, flecks of gold were added; hence the name. Something of a curiosity today.

Irish Mist, 're-invented' in 1948 in Tullamore Distillery; a honey-herbal infusion with Irish whiskey.

Izarra, aromatic Basque liqueur based on Armagnac.

Kahlua, a splendid, not very powerful, Mexican liqueur with a strong coffee flavour.

Royal Mint Chocolate, best known of a range of Royal Mint liqueurs; a liquid and alcoholic 'After Eight'.

Sabra, a splendid newcomer from Israel, compounded from Jaffa oranges and chocolate on a good spirit base. It is packed in an elegant version of an ancient Phœnician wine flask. The name (cactus) is applied to native-born Jewish citizens.

Southern Comfort, because in its homeland, the USA, this is used much as a Bourbon might be, it is mentioned under Spirits. In Europe it is earning popularity as a liqueur, in which category I think it is correctly placed.

Tia Maria, extremely popular Jamaican liqueur, not rum-based but made from rectified cane sugar distillate flavoured with a concentrate of the famous Blue Mountain coffee.

Trappistine, owes something to Bénédictine, but the base is Armagnac, not Cognac.

Van der Hum, the Afrikaans roughly translates as 'What's-'is-name', the South African inventor's name having been forgotten. It is tangerine flavoured.

Vieille Cure, 'the old rectory'; it is made by monks near Bordeaux. Both Cognac and Armagnac are used, and local herbs. A high quality product.

General styles of cordial liqueur, made by more than one firm either under their own name or registered brand name, and also certain alcoholic cordials are:

Advocaat (Advokaat), a Dutch invention, combining brandy, egg yolks, sugar and other ingredients. 'Egg Flip' is not dissimilar but is usually wine-based. Advocaat is popular with the young. In Britain it is often drunk with fizzy lemonade, a Snowball.

Anis, anisette, sweet, aniseed-flavoured cordials of wide geographic manufacture.

Apricot brandies (Abricot), the derivation is obvious.

Crème de Mènthe, deserves separation from other *crèmes*, as it is much less sickly-sweet. It comes in green or white, and the white is the drier. With the best brands, this is an excellent liqueur.

Note: *Crème* usually indicates an extremely sweet drink, more syrup than liqueur or cordial. The French make *crèmes* with many flavours, banana, nut, coffee, raspberry, strawberry, and blackcurrant (*cassis*). *Crème de cassis* should not be confused with the non-alcoholic *cassis* syrup–both are useful flavourings in drinks. (Parfait d'Amour– sweet and brilliantly violet–is a borderline case between a crème and a cordial liqueur.)

Cherry brandy, cherry-flavoured cordial brandy, not to be confused with Kirsch. Cherry Heering is a proprietary cherry-flavoured liqueur.

Ginger wine, bitter-sweet British cordial that goes well with Scotch or brandy.

Kümmel, caraway seed-flavoured plus cummin and aniseed; much esteemed as a digestive by those who can stand caraway. It is sometimes broken down with gin, which cuts the flavour and sweetness.

Kirsch, distilled from cherries, with the stones sometimes crushed to provide a contrast. Not Cherry Brandy, and there's a nice point: if it's a brandy or a liqueur. Derives from the Black Forest, but is made in adjacent countries as well.

Maraschino, at its best is distilled from bitter Dalmatian cherries. An ancient liqueur, appreciated, amongst others, by the Prince Regent. The best comes from Zara on the Adriatic coast, but it is widely copied. Maraschino (cocktail) cherries are, if high quality, steeped in the real liqueur.

Mirabelle, distinctively flavoured with the mirabelle plums of Alsace and Lorraine.

Lemon gin/Orange gin, neither is very widely made or used today, but both are commercially available.

Sloe gin, this is fairly popular and several brands are available. It is also easy to make at home when there is a good sloe crop in the autumn. Half-fill a bottle with individually pricked sloes. Add a level two inches of white sugar. Top the bottle with dry gin. Leave at least three months, shaking once a week. Then taste for sweetness and add more sugar if you wish and leave another month, shaking as before. Decant carefully.

Strega, 'the witch', the popular liqueur of Italy; citrus and herb flavoured. Sometimes taken with ice cream.

There is an infinite variety of cordial/liqueurs. Every region has its own: Yorkshire has its **Bronté**, the Bahamas its excellent **Nassau Royale.** No list can be more than a selection. Always, someone's favourite little liqueur from that lovely spot in the Juras is going to be left out.

Bitters

The term 'bitters' embraces a range of specialised products, and a brand that immediately comes to mind is **Angostura.** This is very widely used in mixed drinks, is what makes 'pink gin' pink, and has culinary virtues. It was evolved in 1824 by Dr J G V Siegert, whose descendants run the company today, in Angostura (now Cuidad Bolivar) in Venezuela. Subsequently production was moved to Trinidad. Angostura has a fairly high alcohol content: 78 proof.

Orange Bitters are rather less employed than formerly, when they were commonly added to sherry. They are part of the equipment of a bar; their use in a Dry Martini cocktail is a matter for debate in professional circles. Bitter Seville orange peel is a prime constituent; around 40 proof.

Much weaker are **Peach Bitters.**

Named as bitters is Campari, but I have listed it properly as an Aperitif.

Amer Picon is a constituent of some cocktails, but it is also used, iced, as a sharp aperitif.

Fernet, of which by far the best known brand is Branca, is largely employed outside Italy for settling queasy stomachs, but in its homeland is drunk as a popular aperitif.

By its taste to be classed as a bitters is **Underberg** (86 proof) of which a million little bottles a day are drunk in West Germany. A bottle is a dose, and I can vouch for its restorative powers.

Syrup

Gomme sirop is a heavy sweetener used by professional bartenders and widely employed in France. It is a mixture of water with pure unrefined cane sugar.

Sugar syrup for home use may be made by boiling the proportions of one pound granulated sugar with one pint water. It can be stored indefinitely under mild refrigeration, and it is more satisfactory in mixed drinks than dry sugar: one uses the same amount of either.

An extremely attractive and useful syrup is **Grenadine,** which is flavoured gently with pomegranate.

Lime juice cordial should perhaps be included here; it is employed part as an additive syrup, part as a non-alcoholic base for a long drink; the best is made simply from fresh lime juice and pure sugar. Not to be confused with the synthetic lime-flavoured drinks which abound.

Hangovers

Since at least two of the drinks I mention under bitters, Fernet and Underberg, have therapeutic qualities, this is as good a place as any to mention the occasional morning sickness to which the word hangover has come to be applied. It is an ugly word; so is the condition.

As to prevention, it has long been believed that milk, cream or oil, taken before drinking on an empty stomach, will reduce the speed of absorption of alcohol into the body, and thus the speed of intoxication, and consequently will reduce the proportions of any hangover. Actual physical research on human guinea-pigs has now proved that certainly the degree of intoxication produced by a given amount of liquor will be lessened, in terms of efficiency, by the ingestion of milk prior to drinking the alcohol. This gives a former old wives' tale scientific authority. Plenty of old wives' tales continue in circulation. For instance, mixing drinks will not make you tighter, but it may induce additional remorse the following morning. Drinking alcohol through a straw has no effect one way or the other. (But speed of drinking, of course, does make for more rapid inebriation.) There seems some evidence that effervescent drinks bring quicker, but not greater, intoxication than a flat one. What you eat, and the fact that you do eat, can make all the difference between matutinal clarity and muzziness. To take lime juice, milk, or just plain water last thing before sleeping, which one rarely remembers to do, together with some anti-acid specific of the seltzer type, is excellent advice.

Regarding cure, time alone is the only remedy, but water and air are helpful, since a hungover person is suffering from a form of minor poisoning in which

lack of oxygen and dehydration are playing their sinister roles. Some swear by Fernet and others (myself included) by Underberg, though in theory the addition of alcohol to an alcoholised system cannot be beneficial. In practice it seems to be, though the good effect may be a mixture of wishful thinking and folk-lore. The 'prairie oyster' is a long esteemed pick-me-up, more breakfast than drink. Mix a little brandy with a teaspoon each of Worcestershire sauce and wine vinegar. Add a dash of pepper. Pour over the yoke of an egg. Ingest the lot in a single swallow. The 'hair of the dog' treatment—though champagne brings illusory relief—cannot be truly recommended except psychologically. The very phrase smacks of alchemy rather than medical science. The Romans believed that if they were bitten by a dog, they would suffer no ill effects if they caught the animal, took some hair from it, burnt the hair and drank it in wine. Obviously, in many cases they did not suffer, thus 'proving' the efficacy of the treatment. If you have a pet cure, and if you believe it works, then it *is* doing you good.

Certain palliative potions, some attractive in their own right, some designed to stun you into consciousness, will be found marked H (hangover) in the Cocktails and Mixed Drinks chapter. This is not necessarily their only use.

To achieve a personal happy medium between enjoyment and excess—for which the word is probably Moderation—must surely be our goal.

Cocktails and mixed drinks

Hereinafter learn all that is known about COCKTAILS

Mixed drinks have been drunk for thousands of years. Much wine of old positively demanded spicing and other mixing to render it palatable. But it is perhaps fanciful to speak of cocktails in relation to antiquity.

I have on occasions listed no fewer than nine possible origins of the odd word cocktail. Here I intend to append the three myths I consider the most probable. One: in the 18th century a horse of mixed blood, as opposed to a thoroughbred, had its tail docked and was said to be 'cock-tailed'–thus a mixture of drinks took its name from hard-drinking equestrian circles. Two: around the same period, at the popular pastime of cock-fighting, there was a custom of toasting a victorious bird in a concoction composed of as many ingredients as it had remaining tail feathers; further, a spirituous mix was fed to fighting cocks to fortify them. Three: a type of mixed wine drink known as *coquetel* was taken to America by Lafayette's troops when they went to support George Washington establish the United States. Certainly the word cocktail was used in an American publication as early as 1806 to describe something we might recognise as a cocktail. Some half a century later the first cocktail book was published, but most cocktails continued to be designated by many specialised names–Crusta, Fix, Daisy, Cobbler, Smash and so on–and not until the 'cocktail age' of the so-called 'roaring 20s' did the word gain universal currency as a general term for mixed drinks. Its definition has been the cause of argument, since a cocktail is exempt from the rules covering the dispensing of spirits in Britain by fixed measures. It is held that three ingredients make a cocktail. But is ice an ingredient? Not all cocktails are chilled; is not water an ingredient? Is a slice of lemon? The matter has not been tested legally.

Classics

There are certain cocktails and related mixed drinks which I define as classics; they have mostly stood the siege of time and changing fashion and are in international use in sophisticated circles. My choice is a personal one. I also include some more recent mixes whose popularity has endured long enough to ensure classic status.

First I would place the **Dry Martini.** I am certain this was evolved in the Knickerbocker Hotel, New York City, around 1910, by Martini di Arma di Taggia, the head bartender. It consisted of dry gin and dry vermouth, in equal proportions, probably with the then much used orange bitters. It was stirred with ice in a mixing glass and then strained into another smaller glass for drinking. This was a revolutionary change from an iced gin-and-French. Today, as any Dry Martini fan knows–and they are legion–it is made in the same way, but with a much lower proportion of vermouth and usually without the bitters. It is customary to press a slice of lemon peel over the finished drink–and I suggest that it be not dropped into it. The immersion of an olive is a matter of personal preference. The same drink with a cocktail onion added is a Gibson, said to be named from a teetotal American ambassador during Prohibition who served his guests drinks but himself carried a glass of water with a pearl onion in it so that people would think he was drinking.

Much lore surrounds the Dry Martini, but here is not the place to repeat it. Suffice it to say that a Dry Martini may correctly nowadays be served 'on the rocks'–traditionally mixed but poured into a glass containing ice cubes. It should always contain dry vermouth, however little, in order to qualify. I know of a Florida bar where a vermouth-less Martini is called a Naked Martini: as it is made with House of Lords gin, is this a tribute to Lord Longford? Vodka is often substituted, on request, for gin, though I feel this makes a less attractive cocktail. I have invented my own Cossacktini for this purpose, using a higher than usual proportion of vermouth to vodka and employing grapefruit in place of lemon rind.

Collins, in popularity this mix outranks the Dry Martini in the USA. The name comes from John Collins, headwaiter at a London hostelry in the early 1800s. The mix became associated with sweet Old Tom gin, which accounts for the use of Tom Collins as a description for it. Today it is properly called John Collins, meaning it is made with London Dry gin, or simply Collins, with the specification that it be made with gin, whisky or brandy. To make: one measure spirit, half-tablespoon sugar, or sugar syrup (qv); juice of half a lemon. Pour over ice cubes in tumbler, and top with soda.

Bronx, one measure dry gin; half-measure each sweet and dry vermouth; juice of quarter-orange. Shake with ice; strain into cocktail glass.

Clover Club, one measure dry gin; half-measure Grenadine syrup; juice of half-lemon; white of one egg. Shake very briskly with ice; strain into wine goblet.

Gimlet, half-and-half dry gin and lime juice cordial; shaken with ice and strained, or served 'on the rocks'; with or without dash of soda.

Gin fizz, one measure dry gin; juice of half-lemon; half-tablespoon sugar or sugar-syrup. Shake well with ice; strain into wine goblet; top with soda.

(Gin) rickey, a Rickey may be made with any spirit, but most frequently it is gin. To make: over ice cubes in tumbler pour two measures spirit; juice of half a lime or lemon; put the crushed half fruit into glass; add a dash of Grenadine syrup; top with soda. See glossary re Rickey.

Gin sling, juice of a lemon; level tablespoon sugar or sugar syrup; two measures dry gin; dash of Angostura bitters. Mix in tumbler with ice and top with water.

Singapore gin sling, two measures dry gin; juice of a lemon; level tablespoon sugar or sugar syrup. Pour over ice cubes in long glass; nearly top with soda. Add half-measure each Cointreau and Cherry Brandy; slice of lemon. Stir. Serve with straws.

Sour, made with any spirit. Two measures preferred spirit; quarter-measure lemon juice; teaspoon sugar or sugar syrup; dash of orange bitters. (Egg white is often used). Shake well with ice, strain into large cocktail glass; soda optional.

Horse's neck, with any spirit. Cut continuous spiral of lemon peel and hang it suspended from rim in tall glass. Add ice; two measures spirit; top with dry ginger ale.

Americano, two measures red vermouth; one measure Campari. Pour over ice in wine-glass; top with soda and add slice of orange. (There are also proprietory ready-made Americanos).

Negroni, as for Americano, plus dry gin.

Silver Streak, one measure dry gin; half-measure each Kümmel and lemon juice; shake with ice and strain. Or may be served with crushed ice (*frappé*).

White Lady, one measure dry gin; half-measure each Cointreau and lemon juice; teaspoon egg white. Shake briskly with ice; strain.

On these pages we see illustrations and recipes from the 'Savoy Cocktail Book', published by Constable in 1930. The decorations are by Gilbert Rumbold, and the recipes by Harry Craddock of the Savoy Hotel.

JABBERWOCK
COCKTAIL.*

2 Dashes Orange Bitters.
⅓ Dry Gin. ⅓ Dry Sherry.
⅓ Caperitif.

Stir well and strain into cocktail glass. Squeeze lemon peel on top.

* This will made you gyre and gimble in the wabe until brillig all right, all right.

Whisky Mac, half-and-half Scotch whisky and ginger wine; not chilled. Brandy Mac is similar, but made with cognac.

Rob Roy, one measure each Scotch whisky and red vermouth. Shake with ice and strain.

Broken Leg, stir in a mug: one measure Bourbon whiskey; 3 measures hot apple juice; 4 raisins; a stick of cinnamon; a slice of lemon.

Highball, probably the name comes from the US railroads. On at least one, in the early days, a ball hoisted high on a post indicated to a driver he'd better put on steam. So the word became connected with speed – and then with a drink easily made and drunk. A Highball, strictly an American term, is any spirit (usually whiskey) with ice and plain or charged water. (Made with cider, it's called a Stone Fence.)

Rusty Nail, half-and-half Scotch whisky and Drambuie; may be served with crushed ice.

Manhattan, despite its title this originated in Maryland and is over a century old. It was a mixture of whiskey, syrup and the then inevitable bitters, but when it emigrated to New York and took a fashionable name the simple syrup was replaced by red vermouth. Now it's a bit more complicated: one measure Bourbon; half-measure each sweet and dry vermouth: dash of Angostura; stir with ice and strain into glass; decorate with cocktail cherry. Can be served 'on the rocks'.

A drawing from a contemporary (1930) French
satirical work which expresses the horror felt by
traditional wine lovers for the cocktail fashion.

102

Mint julep, famous, but scarcely drunk outside the USA. The name *julep* is, oddly, of Persian origin. In the Deep South there is much lore connected with it. A satisfactory recipe is: muddle in a tall glass a lump of sugar, four sprigs of fresh mint, and a tablespoon of water. Almost fill with crushed ice. Add at least two measures of Bourbon whiskey; don't stir; garnish with mint leaves.

Old Fashioned, a dumpy–and extremely useful– tumbler takes its name from this drink. In one of them, stir one teaspoon sugar syrup; two ice cubes; three dashes Angostura; two measures Bourbon whiskey. The stirrer is customarily left in the drink. Add twist of lemon rind and a cocktail cherry.

Bloody Mary (H), capable of infinite variations. Try starting with–two measures vodka; a bottle of tomato juice; dash of celery salt; Tabasco; cayenne pepper; Worcestershire sauce; teaspoon lemon juice. Stir with ice and strain into good-sized glass. Made with tequila instead of vodka this is called Sangre. Made either in the drinking glass or separately.

Bullshot (H), rules, or lack of them, as above. Cold condensed consommé, or strong *boullion,* teaspoon Worcestershire sauce; juice of half-lemon; continue as for Bloody Mary. (An amalgam of both these drinks is a Bloody Bullshot; popular in the USA, and with a big future in Britain when proposed extended licensing hours eventuate!)

Moscow Mule, vodka to own preference with iced ginger beer and slice of lemon.

Screwdriver, fresh orange juice, chilled, spiked with vodka to individual taste. (With Galliano liqueur added, this is the smart American Harvey Wall-banger).

Daiquiri, one measure fine white rum; half-measure each fresh lime (or more of lemon) and Grenadine syrup. Shaken with lots of ice and strained. Serve very cold.

Planter's Punch, the nearest this celebrated drink has to a traditional recipe is the proportion of one sour (lime juice) two sweet (sugar), three strong (rum), four weak (ice and water). However you make it, you stir vigorously and pour the lot into a long glass. You may garnish with grated nutmeg and a slice of fruit, but most experts deplore over-dressing with a lot of citrus garbage. And a lot of connoisseurs change the one, two, three, four order of precedence.

Cuba Libre, white rum and cola; plenty of ice; a little fresh lime (or lemon) juice.

Alexander, one measure each of Cognac, *crème de cacao* and fresh cream. Shake very thoroughly with ice and strain into big cocktail glass.

Sidecar, one measure Cognac; half-measure each Cointreau and lemon juice. Shake with ice; strain.

Margarita, an historic mix, said to date from old Virginia City and to be named for a saloon girl who got shot and died in the arms of her bartender boyfriend who thereafter invented the cocktail. Lately its revival made Tequila fairly a vogue spirit

'It's never too early for a cocktail'.
The Vortex Noël Coward

in parts of the USA. Two measures Tequila; one measure each Cointreau and lime (or lemon) juice. Shake; strain into glass of which rim has been moistened with lemon juice and dipped in salt.

Kir, famous, if only a cocktail by stretching the term. A glass of well chilled white Burgundy, to which a teaspoon of *crème de Cassis* (blackcurrant) has been added. This drink can also be made with dry champagne.

Champagne cocktail, place a lump of sugar in a large wine goblet; add three drops of Angostura bitters and a measure of Cognac. Top with chilled non-vintage Champagne. Slice of orange optional.

Buck's Fizz (H), half-and-half chilled non-vintage Champagne and fresh juice. Today this is a more fashionable drink than Champagne cocktail.

Ready-prepared mixes can be bought: they are more popular in the US than elsewhere. They give the flavour for Sours, Collins, etc–you add the spirit. There are also prepared bottled cocktails: not for me!

Sundry mixed drinks

Atholl Brose, something similar to this with the same name is made up with oatmeal, the result being a kind of alcoholic porridge. A liquid version is: two measures Scotch whisky; one ounce each clear honey and cream. Mix well in warmed glass and let cool. Or serve hot with milk instead of cream as a type of Toddy.

Whisky toddy, with a silver spoon, as custom dictates, dissolve a heaped teaspoon of sugar with a little hot water in a warmed glass. Add two measures of Scotch whisky and stir, pouring in more boiling water. Top with another measure of Scotch.

Irish coffee, put heaped teaspoon sugar in a stemmed glass; add plenty of Irish whiskey and dissolve sugar. Pour in strong, hot coffee. Cover with fresh cream carefully poured over the back of a spoon. Do not stir it. Most spirits may be added to coffee, though not usually with cream as well.

Nog (nogg), the basic Egg Nog is any hot sugared spirit with egg blended well into it. Made with beer instead of spirit it is a Flip. A favourite is Rum Nog, particularly in the USA. which would usually have milk as well and be topped with a little grated nutmeg. Nogs may be chilled or taken (medicinally) hot.

Yankee Invigorator (H), an elaborate Nog. Beat an egg in shaker or blender; add half-pint strong cold coffee; one measure brandy; half-glass port; sugar to taste. Blend well with ice and strain into large goblet.

Stinger, two measures Cognac; one measure white *crème de menthe*. Shake well with ice, and strain.

Bishop, an individual version of an extremely varied drink. This old US recipe says: dissolve in long glass tablespoon sugar with juice of half an orange, a little lemon juice and half a glass soda; half fill with ice and top with Burgundy. Stir, and add a little dark rum and fruit as available.

Sangaree, sangria, an old, famous drink, much revived. Traditionally, a little sugar dissolved with any preferred wine, ice, and topped with the same wine. If served hot and with red wine, a little grated nutmeg is added. Today it is essentially a chilled wine drink with a good deal of fruit added.

Black Russian, half-and-half vodka and Kahlua, the Mexican coffee liqueur. Serve 'on the rocks'.

Black Velvet (H), half-and-half Guiness and chilled non-vintage champagne. Best served in tankard.

Syllabub, on the fringe between food and drink. To make this old English dish: per portion – two measures sweet sherry, one ounce each double cream and milk; teaspoon powdered sugar. Blend, tasting to adjust sweetness. (At least this is one use for those beastly saucer champagne glasses! They are just right for serving this – with teaspoons.)

The well-known fashions and styles of the cocktail era.

Some party drinks (hot and cold)

Champagne punch (16 servings), two bottles inexpensive dry champagne; four measures brandy; four measures Cointreau; four measures Maraschino. Mix the liqueurs; add the champagne, very cold and iced soda-water. No ice in the bowl. Decorate with fruit. A substitute can satisfactorily be made with *brut* sparkling wine. Serve chilled in stemmed glasses.

Sherry punch (22 servings), one bottle medium sherry; one bottle brandy; two bottles dry effervescent wine; siphon soda; teaspoon each Cointreau and Maraschino. Mix all except wine in bowl with ice. Add fruit as available. Add chilled wine at last minute. Serve in stemmed glasses.

English Bishop (8 servings), stick an orange with a dozen cloves and brown in oven. Cut into quarters and place in large saucepan. Pour in one bottle port. Heat gently, stirring in brown sugar to required degree of sweetness. Cover and allow to heat for half an hour: it must not boil. Add rum, brandy, cinnamon and nutmeg at personal discretion. Serve in small handled glasses or mugs. This can be the basis for various Punches, using red wine as well as port; the mutations are endless.

Glogg (14 servings), bottle each of medium sherry and red wine; about three ounces brown sugar; eight dashes Angostura; half-bottle brandy. Heat without boiling. Put into warmed mugs a few raisins and an almond each (not salted). Pour the heated brew on top.

Tea punch (12 servings), half-bottle each of dark rum and brandy; half-pound sugar; one quart very strong tea (strained); juice of a lemon. Heat together slowly, without boiling. There is an elaborate version of this calling for setting the mixture on fire: such practice can only burn out the alcohol.

White wine punch (24 servings), one pint sugar syrup; pint and a half lemon juice (unsweetened, bottled); bottle of dry sherry; three bottles dry white wine; half-bottle brandy; half-pint strong strained tea. Mix in large jug(s) and refrigerate. Before serving, add soda-water and decorate with rounds of cucumber and/or fruit.

Cider cup (14 servings), a flagon of (still) dry cider; half-pint (canned) orange juice; juice of a lemon; small glass of Cointreau. Chill cider and mix with other ingredients. Before serving, add siphon soda, a few ice cubes and slices of orange and lemon. (Add gin or vodka with discretion for extra kick). This can be adapted for White Wine Cup, in which case fortify with brandy.

Mull, any wine, beer, plus spirits or not, heated: usually with spices and sugar.

Hints and equipment

So far as possible, all bulk drinks should be made up experimentally in a small quantity first; you can then adjust taste, and simple arithmetic will allow you to make any quantity you require. A great deal of work can be done ahead of the entertainment and stored in bottles, under refrigeration if necessary. For fairly large scale entertainment you may need to buy ice. Increasingly one can purchase bags of ice-cubes; in a cool place they will keep, without undue melting, for twenty-four hours or more. Never add effervescent wines or mineral waters to drinks until the last moment or they'll go flat.

A lot of the individual cocktails I've outlined can, of course, be made in fair quantities and stored.

You don't need a home cocktail bar–though my correspondence indicates these are becoming more and more popular–in order to make mixed drinks at home. The basic cocktail equipment is neither elaborate nor expensive. But naturally one thing leads to another, and there are plenty of fascinating gadgets for the man who gets hooked as an amateur mixologist: electric blenders (essential for a frozen Daiquiri), ice crushers, ice-makers–all the professional knick-knacks are available for domestic mix-it-yourself devotees. However, all you need to start with are: a mixing glass, either with built-in strainer or, preferably, a separate Hawthorne strainer; a long bar spoon for mixing. Next comes a shaker. I suggest a three-piece one in plain stainless steel. It must fit together well. Always wrap a cloth round, for vigorous shaking may cause leaks. A mixing glass is used for stirring cocktails not containing heavy syrups and cordials or ingredients like egg white. Shakers are more or less essential for drinks with disparate constituents like spirit and liqueur, that can't really be blended successfully by mixing in a glass.

It is surprising how little else you really *need* to be in the mixing business. I think you will find extremely useful an ice bowl (insulated), a sharp serrated fruit knife, and a robust lemon-juice extractor (not a fancy electrified one to start with). Large glass jugs are important: a big punch bowl is a luxury, but a splendid one. It is almost too obvious to point out that you need to have to hand the gin, whisky, other spirits you may want, vermouths, and such things as Grenadine and Maraschino cherries. Always keep a few lemons around. The amateur should check his stock occasionally for items like soda and fruit juices as well as basic liquors and the usual mineral waters. The more exotic cordials and liqueurs can be bought in small sizes.

As to glasses: don't try to use very small cocktail glasses, nor emulate the habit of some cocktail bars of filling them brim-full, but rather a somewhat larger stemmed glass, two-thirds filled. It looks more pleasant, presents less problems for possibly shaky-handed topers, and may cause less damage to polished furniture. Glasses chilled in the 'fridge improve the presentation of such cocktails as Dry Martini and Daiquiri. Tumblers, tall 12-oz. glasses, and normal wine glasses are the only other basic glass requirements for a domiciliary bartender. For hot drinks, insulated drinking vessels are excellent, but glass-handled mugs are more decorative. Recently I found what might be the perfect party glass—you hang it round your neck and when not imbibing you have both hands free! This brainwave comes from Denmark.

Reverting to wine, in connection with equipment, I would reiterate the importance of a really good corkscrew. An ice-bucket need not be expensive and is highly decorative—some could double as a punch bowl. Neither need claret jugs or simple carafes be costly; there are even some old ones to be found if you keep your eyes open in junk shops. A well designed carafe has many purposes: for decanting wine table wines into, for serving bulk wines, or for serving prepared mixed drinks at parties. Good decanters that also pour well are essential. And don't forget that gadget for closing half-used bottles of sparkling wine. There is some excellent equipment made at all price levels, but avoid the fancy, over-decorated; go for the well-designed and sensible.

Opposite Professor Jeremy Thomas, bartender of the past, mixing his famous 'Blue Blazer' at the Metropolitan Hotel, New York.

Above An illustration from a French satirical work of 1931—'Modern Dialogue in three Acts and three Cocktails', by René Benjamin.

Mainly soft drinks

I will be candid: this chapter gives me more trouble to write than any other. But in researching it I have learned a lot.

There are a huge number of soft drinks which are attractive for entertaining–to amuse the kids, and flatter your temperance friends, who are often too little considered whilst the boozers enjoy themselves. And a number of drinks are not just calorific but positively nutritional and, in their non-alcoholic way, exhilarating. (I do mention the addition of alcohol as an optional extra in specific instances, where this is a logical stimulation.) I have included a few brand-names, as these often cannot be avoided without tautology.

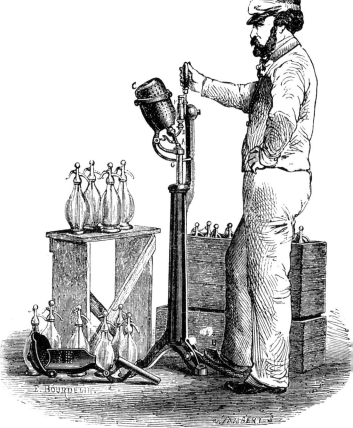

Carbonated soft drinks

Medicinal springs, producing naturally carbonated water, enjoy a fame going back almost before recorded history. Some springs are of comparatively recent fame, but many that are household names today were in use in antiquity, though it was not then practicable to take the water to the drinker; it was exclusively the other way about. The Romans knew about them though they used them more for bathing than for internal use–witness Bath. Spas, named for the German town of Spa–noted for its curative mineral waters–in due course became fashionable, the well-to-do frequenting them hope-fully to undo the ravages of gourmandising. Nowa-days spas, with a few exceptions, have declined, but waters such as Vichy, Evian, San Pellegrino, and Perrier, have become important industries; just these four spas produce still, semi-sparkling, effervescent, and both tasteless and mineral-flavoured waters. To imitate such 'mineral' waters–so called for their mineral content–was a widely shared ambition. The word has latterly come to be generally applied to tonic-water, bitter-lemon, and the like. There is no longer any point in copying spa waters since they can be transported anywhere.

The discovery of the constituents of the bubbles in effervescent waters was made by a Belgian in the 16th century, but not until 1772 did a British scientist, Joseph Priestly, succeed in producing artificially carbonated water (according to the National Association of Soft Drinks Manufacturers). He made it in barrels. The next stop was to add flavour to the carbonated water. The most successful was lime juice and this came to be used throughout the Royal Navy to stop sailors getting scurvy from their vitamin-deficient diet.

Nicholas Paul of Geneva is credited with starting to manufacture imitation spa waters in bulk in 1789. One of his partners, Jacob Schweppe, came to England about four years later and started making soda-water. Next to his factory he had a pharmacy where he sold this preparation, for soda- or seltzer-waters were medicinal. The idea of mixing them with other things–hock was possibly the first of these–came much later. This is emphasised by the fact that mineral waters were taxed as patent medicines at the high rate of threepence a bottle. Schweppe was able to retire on his profits in 1799; what was to become an industrial giant became a public company in 1897; its products need no extra boost from me. Schweppes market, amongst many other products, the natural aerated mineral water from Germany (Apollinaris) and Malvern Water, and are pro-prietors of the premier lime juice, Rose's.

The principal ingredients of all carbonated waters are water, carbon dioxide (CO_2), sugar, fruit juice and/or synthetic flavouring. An early step in manu-facture is to demineralise the water, rendering it completely sterile. The CO_2 not only makes the water fizzy; it gives it durability under all conditions.

The sugar may be either cane or beet; there has recently been trouble about some synthetic sweetners, but saccharin is permitted.

Most fruit used is citrus. It comes from a score of countries, usually processed where it is grown. It is squeezed and concentrated to up to six times its natural strength and must be stored under refrigera-tion. Another method of using fruit is by commin-ution: for this, the whole fruit is employed, including the peel. (It may here be worth digressing to state that in British law a fruit squash always contains a

regulation proportion of juice only; a fruit drink is composed of a controlled amount of comminuted whole fruit. That is the difference.)

Next, bottling. If non-returnable, bottles will come direct from the manufacturers; if returnables, they will be most carefully washed and sterilised. On the bottling lines tiny amounts of concentrated flavouring –which in bulk you would not recognise for what they are–are automatically dropped into each bottle, carbonated water is added and the bottles are immediately capped and labelled. All this is done at devastating speed. Soda-water has nothing added but a trace of bicarbonate of soda. Siphons are, incidentally, re-charged through the spout.

In Britain nearly 500 firms manufacture soft drinks. Including an allowance for dilution of squashes, fruit drinks and fruit-based syrups and cordials, about 625 million gallons of soft drinks are consumed annually, and expenditure on these products runs at well over £200 million. The trade is strictly regulated as to hygiene and quality of ingredients used in production.

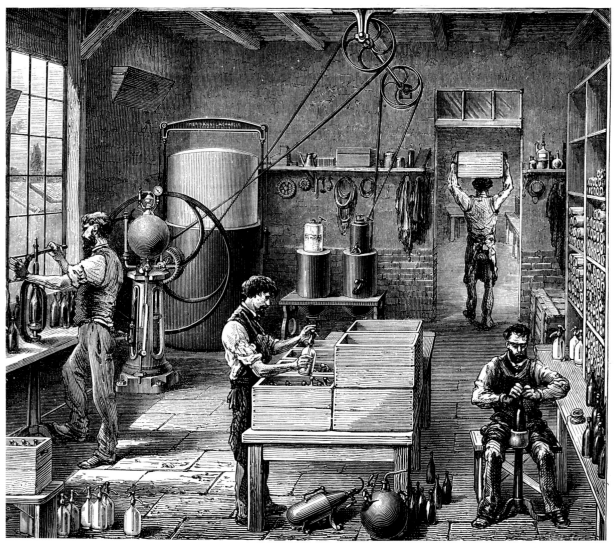

Opposite The manufacture of soda-water in France and a siphon for 'acidulated water'.
Right This impressive example of modern technology is a portion of the complex machinery of a soft drinks manufacturing plant.
Below The natural Jaffa orange juice goes to the automatic can- and bottle-filling machines.

In the USA the equivalent market is over 3,000 million gallons for the top selling ten brands alone! The per capita consumption of all soft drinks runs at 560 8-oz. bottles per year for every man, woman and child in the country. **Coca-Cola** have an astounding 34 per cent of this vast market.

One can hardly write properly on soft drinks without saying something about this product. New Coca-Cola bottling plants (under franchise) open at the rate of one a fortnight somewhere in the world. Whilst this rate has declined in recent years, this is not due to a reduction in the rate of growth of the product. The reason is that as new, bigger and more modern plants are built, they can handle the production capacity of a smaller number of earlier plants. More than 150 million drinks of Coca-Cola are consumed daily. During the war Coke was available to American troops in every combat zone at 5 cents a bottle; 5,000 million were distributed. Coke originated as a friendly name for Coca-Cola.

1887
Second Home of Coca-Cola
No. 2 Marietta Street
Southwest Corner Marietta and Peachtree Streets at Five Points

Jacobs' Pharmacy at Five Points, which housed Willis E. Venable's soda fountain. Here Coca-Cola syrup was manufactured from July, 1887, to December, 1887. On December 14, 1887, Messrs. Lowndes and Venable sold their interests in Coca-Cola to Walker, Candler & Company, composed of Woolfolk Walker, Dr. Joseph Jacobs and Asa G. Candler. The equipment was moved back to its original location at 107 Marietta Street and Coca-Cola was again manufactured there until early September, 1888.

Left A refreshing drink of Coca-Cola.
Below and opposite Bottling and crating of soft drinks in a British firm.
Top opposite A soft drink enjoyed at high speed—not, one would imagine, ideal circumstances under which to partake of refreshment.

It was registered as a Trade Mark by The Coca-Cola Company as long ago as 1920. And it all started in 1886 when it was first sold in Atlanta, Georgia by its inventor, Dr. John S. Pemberton, a Pharmacist, who in that year invested $46 out of sales revenue of $50 on advertising. The base is a secret formula syrup, to which sugar and carbonated water are added. Once the syrup was only made in Atlanta, but is now made by The Coca-Cola Company at a number of overseas plants.

Coke is not the only cola by any means. Its principal rival is equally well-known **Pepsi-Cola,** with about 15 per cent of the American soft drink market but seriously rivalling Coke in some other countries. This started a trifle later, when Caleb (Doc) Bradham put out a stimulating thirst-quencher in New Bern, North Carolina. It was known as Brad's Drink locally. Bradham thought up the title Pepsi-Cola and registered it in 1903. By 1916 a hundred bottlers had franchises for the drink. The Depression saw Pepsi start a forward surge, for it reduced its price and made great headway during that period. I regret to record that it also invented the singing radio commercial!

A not dissimilar American product is **7-Up,** with a sale about half that of Pepsi's; this is gaining some strength overseas. These three leaders are all used on their own or with the white rum or vodka now

fashionable with young drinkers. Cola has lately been promoted as an excellent mixer with gin, with Booth's pioneering this pleasing innovation.

Of mineral waters, I think **tonic** must generically be the best-known. It started life as Indian quinine water, and was a combination of a social drink and the obligatory quinine taken by imperial admini-strators in malaria-infested climes. (It later made the reputation of Schweppes and did great things for gin). A great many firms make it today, and in France, on its own, it is highly fashionable; they don't call it tonic–simply use the name of the world-famous makers. The French have themselves brought out a beverage with much the same taste, Gini.

Opposite Here we see a prime example of American soft drink influence, an influence often deplored by those who down their colas with relish. Certainly one can get one's Cokes or Pepsis or Schweppes in Singapore, but the old ways die hard, and a Chinaman is still more likely to pause at a kerbside stall, such as the one illustrated *(below)*, and imbibe a refreshing bowl of steaming tea.

I regret that one simply can't get old-style English brewed **ginger beer,** very gingery and very fizzy. Those of maturer years will remember this product as coming in a stoneware bottle with a wired-on cork.

Ginger ale is very much drunk. I understand it was invented in Ireland by a doctor Cochrane; he went in with a Cantrell, and the main line of the resultant firm make the Club range of minerals. The leading name in this field is Canada Dry, who introduced Britain to American ginger ale–sweeter than the usual dry ginger. That company also make an 'extra' which is sharper and more like the tangy pre-war dry ginger ale which has virtually disappeared.

For economy and convenience of transport, particularly on the continent of Europe, more and more use is being made of big plastic bottles for spa and mineral waters, fruit drinks and other beverage drinks, including the more ordinary French table wines. This is not an innovation anywhere regarded with favour environmentally.

A word about plastic. There have been lengthy experiments in its employment for bottles of better wines, fortified wines, and spirits, particularly in relation to airlines. It is now conceded that wines can be satisfactorily stored in the special hard plastics that have been evolved and they are acceptable for neutral spirits like vodka. However, at the moment only some Scotch whisky houses consider plastic satisfactory; there remains a danger that, in prolonged storage, the flavour of the spirit could be damaged. This problem will probably be surmounted. But where weight considerations are not of importance, for quality potables, soft or hard, no material can rival the qualities of glass nor is likely to.

As opposed to squashes or fruit drinks, to be diluted with water or soda or otherwise mixed, there are straight bottled fruit juices–orange predominating–for drinking on their own or with spirits. They are normally sold in small one-drink bottles since, as a natural product (with only sugar added, if that)

Above Opening of the first public drinking fountain in London.

Opposite A water seller in Marrakesh, where fresh running water is not such an accepted fact of life as it is in Britain and America.

118

they will not, unlike concentrated squashes, keep once opened. Tomato juice is also thus sold. There are also larger canned sizes of most juices – and I recommend turning them into jugs (not retaining them in metal) and storing in the 'fridge if they are not all used at one time.

There is now available a good selection of pure apple and grape juice. They are both admirable chilled. Especially in its unsweetened form, pure bottled lemon juice is a most useful bar adjunct.

Did you know there was such a thing as non-alcoholic wine: I don't mean grape juice, but wine? "Wunderbar" is such a product, either red or white, produced from Rhine wines. The wine is fermented normally, and by a patented process the alcohol is then extracted. So the result has all vinous attributes, bar the alcohol.

For a flavoured sweetner in any drink we may raid the nursery; both pure rose-hip and blackcurrant syrups (the latter not to be confused with 'black-currant' flavour) can play a big role in a selection of interesting alcoholic or non-alcoholic drinks. Personally, I would never be without blackcurrant syrup. There is one exotic fruit juice that I would strongly advocate, if you can find it: that is passion fruit.

Quick lemonade, a very simple one is made by taking the juice of a lemon, two teaspoons of sugar; pour into glass of crushed ice; top with water or soda; add a slice of lemon and serve with straws.

Much more interesting is:

Home-made lemonade (3 servings), one large lemon; 4-ozs. granulated sugar; 1½ pints boiling water; one level desertspoon citric acid (available from any chemist). Squeeze juice from lemon; peel rind thinly. Put juice, peel, sugar and citric acid in a jug and pour on boiling water. Stir. Allow to cool. By doubling the quantities of lemon, sugar and citric acid but not the water, you can make a lemonade which can be stored in the 'fridge and diluted as and when required.

'Mocktails'

To cocktails made without alcohol, years ago I gave the name mocktails.

Pussyfoot, a classic, no fixed recipe, but a third each of fresh lemon, fresh orange, and lime juice will do for a start; dash of Grenadine, (and half-teaspoon sugar if lime juice happens to be unsweetened). Yolk of an egg. Shake well with ice and strain into wine goblet. Top with soda and serve with cocktail cherry.

Limey, one measure lime juice cordial; half-measure fresh lemon juice; teaspoon egg white. Shake vigorously with ice, and strain.

Yellow Dwarf, measure each of cream and almond syrup; yolk of an egg. Shake briskly with ice and strain; top up with splash of soda.

Slim Jim, two measures each tomato juice and fresh unsweetened grapefruit juice; half-teaspoon Worcestershire sauce. Shake with ice and strain into goblet.

Tomato mocktail, a Bloody Mary (qv) without the vodka.

Longer drinks

Apple Tankard, three-quarters fill a pint tankard with apple juice (chilled); add juice of an orange and slices of orange, apple, lemon and other fruit in season, plus a few ice cubes.

White Angel punch (30 servings), half-pint sugar syrup, two pints strong, strained tea, one bottle unsweetened lemon juice, two bottles pure grape juice, two siphons soda. Mixed chilled ingredients, plus a little ice, adding soda at last moment, plus fruit in season for decoration.

Nicholas, was invented for one of the author's grandsons, Nicholas Maasz, by well-known London bartender Tommy Langley. It consists of equal, and fairly large, quantities of fresh orange juice, lemon juice and lime juice cordial plus a measure of grenadine syrup and a teaspoon of egg white. Shake up with crushed ice until thoroughly chilled and strain into a tall glass.

These enticing drinks illustrated are, in fact, cocktails, not 'mocktails'. From left to right they are: Horse's Neck (gin based), Blood and Sand (whisky based), Bullshot (vodka based), Dry Martini (gin based), Champagne cocktail (brandy based), Daiquiri (rum based), Negroni (gin based), Manhattan (whisky based), Bloody Mary (vodka based) and Atholl Brose (whisky based).

A large bowl of punch or wine cup always goes
well at a party, though not everyone has such
fine silver in which to serve it.

Tea

you can certainly drink the world's worst cup of tea in Britain; a situation analogous to the fact that one can get as abominable a glass of wine in France as anywhere.

There is such a difference between the China and Indian types of tea, with subtle sub-divisions in each, that I feel choice must be left to individual taste. (I happen to have a preference for rather strong, dark tea, which is not considered good form in esoteric tea-drinking circles!) The slimming craze has certainly brought a revival of Russian tea – without milk and plus a slice of lemon. Iced tea is delicious: for this, I suggest making the tea the way you like it hot – then refrigerating it.

Iced milk tea, instead of infusing with water, use boiling milk or a mixture of milk and water. Sweeten to taste, strain, and refrigerate. If you are going to use ice cubes, make the tea extra strong.

Since tea is a prime ingredient of the above party punch, this is the place to say something about it. At a date unknown the *thea* plant was introduced into China, probably from Korea: the Chinese called it *tcha*. It was introduced in Japan, too. In East India Company correspondence of 1615 it is referred to as *chaw* and an earlier Portuguese writer called it *chia*. By 1650 it was being sold in London at £10–£15 a pound, an enormous price. It continued to be fairly expensive for a long time – those lovely lock-up caddies were not meant just to be decorative. The East India Company's monopoly of trade with China ended in 1883, and the price of tea started to fall; the introduction of Indian tea growing a few years later caused a revolution in attitudes to tea, and its price fell dramatically so that it became the national drink of the British.

It has long been a British belief that you can't get a decent cuppa (tea) outside the UK. In practice,

An English family at tea, a painting by Joseph van Aken. The oldest recorded silver teapot, presented by the East India Company to George Berkley.

Here the blended tea is being tasted by an expert.
Years of experience are necessary for this job.

Tea picking in Ceylon, and sorting the leaves after bringing them in from the fields.

Above A Moroccan family enjoys a glass of coffee.
Top The English tea-drinking habit, depicted by an anonymous artist of the 18th century.
Right The tea plant in flower.

Maté

Locally, various herbal infusions replace tea, socially or medicinally, but the only one that is at all widely known is Maté, the popular beverage drink of much of South America. It is available in other parts of the world, and I have found it extremely refreshing and stimulating.

Actually, maté is the name of the traditional bowl, once a simple gourd but developed into an art form, from which maté is drunk through a tube with a strainer at the end. Sometimes also referred to as Paraguayan tea, the herb, yerba, is a type of holly—*ilex Paraguayansis*. I think it only needs a little promotion to create a vogue for this attractive and seemingly healthful drink. It is normally taken piping hot, but it could certainly be adapted as a basis for a chilled drink.

Opposite Two stages in the production of tea: weighing the freshly picked tea leaves, and pouring them into large troughs where they will be sorted.
Right The plant *Ilex Paraguayensis*, more commonly known as *maté,* which is actually the special bowl (illustrated) from which this very popular South American infusion is drunk through a *bombilla*, a tube with a filtering device at its extremity.
Below Argentinians relaxing with their traditional drink of *maté*.

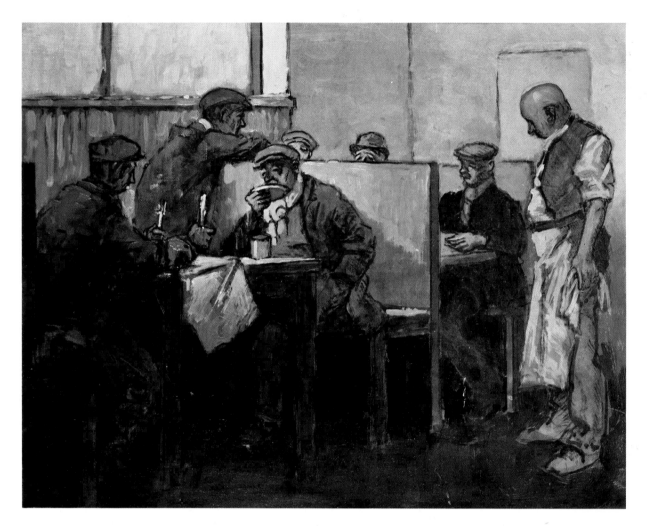

This painting, done about 1960, shows lorry drivers having a meal in a coffee shop. This type of cheap eating house, with back-to-back seating, was common in Victorian and Edwardian London. The still-life *(above)* shows a more elegant and sophisticated approach to coffee drinking.

A flight of fancy by the tea industry in 1899.

Coffee

Coffea Arabica is indigenous to Abyssinia and Arabia, which are certainly two countries which the average consumer would not identify as a commercial source of coffee. He would be right: coffee took a long time to reach Western Europe. In London it was first purveyed by a Greek in 1652. It became a craze in the world of fashion. In France and in the United States—and many other countries—it became the everyday drink. In Britain, tea assumed that position. Today tea is enormously drunk in the USA and increasingly in France, and coffee (frequently instant coffee) is universal in the UK. Again, we witness the breaking-down of purely national beverage patterns.

I see no cause to despise instant coffee. I rate it a much better invention than the pre-mixed cocktail! It is extremely convenient, and not all alleged 'convenience' foods/beverages can justify that description. However, I imagine not even instant brand-owners would rate their products superior to freshly-roasted, newly-ground coffee. The methods of making are as various as the types of coffee themselves. If you wish to conserve the full aroma, an enclosed system—as opposed to a straightforward

infusion with boiling water—is preferable. There are many styles of apparatus, I think the Cona principal is best, but that is only an expression of personal opinion. Steam (espresso) machines—domestic or commercial—extract everything from the beans: this may make too acid a brew for you.

I have the equipment for making Turkish coffee, but have never succeeded satisfactorily in producing this delightful style. You don't have to have the special saucepan; any one will do. You buy the special powdered coffee which specialised shops provide. For two, you will need $1\frac{1}{2}$ small cups of water (of the size you will be serving the beverage in); 2 heaped teaspoons sugar. Boil, and throw in 1 heaped tablespoon coffee. Boil up three times. Remove from flame and drop in a sprinkling of cold water. Remove any froth and pour very carefully. Theoretically the grounds should have sunk to the bottom—though mine never do.

Iced coffee is particularly delicious. In French cafés it is usually made simply by pouring strong hot coffee on to ice cubes and sugaring to taste: you can elaborate as much as you care to. Blending with ice cream produces an attractive version.

129

Top A coffee house of 1674, an early illustration to a broadsheet on coffee.

Top right Morning coffee in the late 18th or early 19th century, showing a type of pot still repeated today.

Above Advertisement for sundry coffee and chocolate-pots of patent design around seventy years ago, and *right,* a superb French coffee-pot of about 1780.

130

Top Picking coffee, and *right* using water canals to move fresh coffee in Costa Rica.
Above right It may surprise you that these coffee-making machines are in operation nowhere more exotic than London's Knightsbridge.
Above A London coffee-stall.

Other beverages

Cocoa (cacao, coco), we get chocolate from this. The original Mexicans called it *chocolatl* from choco (cocoa) latl (water). It came to Europe before coffee or tea. Drinking chocolate is widely popular. The old-fashioned cocoa which one had to make is really the same thing but not quite as easy to prepare. Try this on a warm day:

Chocolate frappé, (4 servings): 8 tablespoons drinking chocolate; 4 tablespoons water; $1\frac{1}{4}$ pints cold milk; $\frac{1}{8}$ pint cream. Dissolve chocolate in hot water; whisk in the milk. Top with cream, lightly whipped. Chill, without freezing.

There is a range of patent beverages of the malted milk type and it would be invidious to mention some and omit others. Essentially, they are palatable hot health drinks, sustaining for the delicate and soporific for the robust. Several are delicious served cold and are quite suitable for use as al fresco summer hospitality.

CADBURY'S COCOA

*"The typical Cocoa of English manufacture:
absolutely pure."*—THE ANALYST.

NO CHEMICALS USED (as in many of the so-called pure Foreign Cocoas).

Milk

I have already mentioned milk in Chapter 4 in connection with drink, and I will here establish a closer link between milk and the hard stuff.

Tiger's Milk, teaspoon sugar syrup; 2 measures brandy; teaspoon egg white; drop of vanilla extract and pinch of powdered cinnamon. Beat egg with the syrup, vanilla and cinnamon. Shake this with ice plus the brandy. Strain into a goblet and fill with a mixture of sweet cider and milk. Sprinkle a little powdered nutmeg on top.

Milk punch, an egg, half-pint milk, 3 teaspoons sugar syrup. Shake well with ice and strain into large glass, dusting with powdered nutmeg. This is the Prohibition version: any desired liquor may be added, Scotch, rum, or brandy being the best.

Puff, make as for Milk punch but use less milk and after straining into glass, top with soda-water and stir lightly.

Milk combines particularly well with whisky: I know of a club where a double Scotch with milk is the most favoured drink with members. The bar carries a notice saying 'Milk's all right—with Black & White'.

Milk chocolate rum, 1 cup hot milk, 2 teaspoons drinking chocolate, 3 teaspoons dark rum. Briskly stir ingredients into the milk.

But this is primarily a non-alcoholic section so I'll revert to temperance.

Country milk-shake, (3 servings), pint of milk, tablespoon rose-hip syrup, a small carton of ice cream. Whisk (or shake with ice) and sprinkle with coloured sugar crystals if you have them, or with a little granulated brown sugar.

For the children

Festival frappé, 1 (mashed) banana; 2 tablespoons bramble jelly; quarter-pint milk, brickette of dairy ice cream. Whisk together banana, jelly, and milk; cut ice cream into cubes and blend in. Serve in tall glass with spoon.

Top opposite A lady of fashion sips chocolate, a popular drink in the 18th century.
Bottom opposite The girls in this painting by Cayley Robinson seem much in need of their bedtime bowl of hot milk.

Miscellaneous non-alcoholic drinks

First aid, juice of a lemon; teaspoon sugar; tablespoon Ribena blackcurrant syrup. Mix in tumbler with crushed ice; top with soda and slice of lemon.

Mint cooler, crush two sprigs of fresh mint with tablespoon powdered sugar in a tumbler; decorate with spiral of lemon peel and top with fizzy lemonade.

Cassis-soda, three measures blackcurrant cordial in tall glass with ice cubes; tablespoon lemon juice; top with soda.

Ingenuity needs be shown to make non-alcoholic drinks, amusing and palatable. It's worth looking at the appropriate shelves in major supermarkets or specialised stores—new fruit products are constantly coming on to the market. Be careful to watch for notices on cans of fruit juice indicating whether they are natural or sweetened, for it makes all the difference in making up drinks; you don't want to sweeten something already very sweet.

From time to time I have made use of flavourless food colourings. A drop added to the water in your ice tray produces chromatic cubes which add visual impact to colourless mixes.

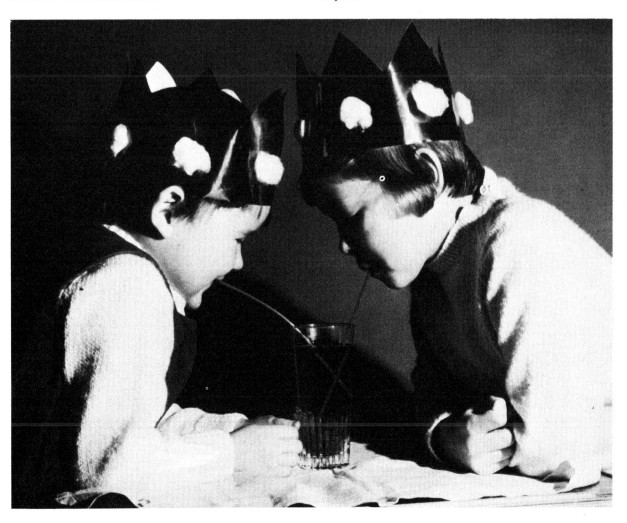

Glossary

Glossary, in alphabetical form, of some terms used in the world of drinks and drinking, together with elaboration of matters elsewhere referred to, and some incidental information which does not logically fall under a particular chapter heading. This section should be used in conjunction with the Index.

Abbocato Sweet (Italian)

Age There are two types with wine— wood (cask) age; and bottle (matured) age—eg vintage ports, clarets, burgundies. With spirit only wood age counts: there is no improvement, or deterioration, in bottle.

Alcohol Absolute (pure) alcohol is 175·25 proof (British); 200 proof (American); 100 Gay Lussac (metric). Potable (drinking) alcohol is called ethyl alcohol; industrial,

sometimes called 'wood', alcohol, is known as methyl alcohol (methanol) and is poisonous. For special purposes, potable alcohol may be treated (methylated) which makes it very disagreeable to drink, but dipsomaniacs will imbibe it and it becomes addictive and eventually lethal. See **Proof.**

Amarone The best Valpolicella, which, comparatively rare amongst Italian wines, may be vintage wine.

Aperitif Any stimulant appetizer; see

Barrels appropriate section Chapter 2. More traditional than actual, beer barrel sizes in Britain are in gallons, butt–108; puncheon–72; hogshead–54; Barrel–36; kilderkin–18; firkin–9; pin–4½. For wine and most spirits the term cask (qv) usually applies.

Bond Government controlled duty-free store. Distilleries and breweries are 'bonded'.

Bottles: sizes The standard British spirit bottle contains 26·6 fluid ounces (1⅓ pints) which is known in the USA as a 'fifth' (one fifth of a US gallon). An American quart is 33·3 British fluid ounces. Considerably in use is the British 40 oz bottle, an imperial quart. The average wine bottle is 0·75 litres, virtually the same as the American fifth. A brandy bottle for the British market is smaller, 24 fluid ounces.
Wine bottle sizes vary marginally for different styles. A magnum is a double-bottle, and double magnums (jeroboams) are sold.
Other, semi-legendary bottles, with biblical names whose origins are lost, are Rehoboam, 6 bottles; Methuselah, 8; Salamanazar, 12; Balthazar, 16; Nebuchanezzar, 20. Only very exceptionally are such giants made, and then only for Champagne. Wine matures more slowly and keeps longer in larger containers; witness the fact that quarter-bottles of Champagne often go prematurely flat.
See also **Metrication.**

Brut Used to describe very dry Champagnes and other sparkling wines. Sometimes emphasised as *brut de brut* (none drier).

Casks The commonest wine and spirit casks in gallons are butt (Scotch)–108; barrel (American and Canadian whisky)–48 (US); puncheon (rum)–100; hogshead (rum)–56; pipe (port)–115; puncheon (brandy)–120; butt (sherry)–108; hogshead (sherry)–54; *barrique* (Bordeaux)–50 (known as *pièce* in Burgundy); *doppleohm* (Germany)–65. See Barrels.

Chambré A wine rested in a room to achieve room temperature.

Charring Slightly burning the interior of spirit casks used to mature many whiskies.

Clos	Burgundy term for vineyard, meaning it was, or is, enclosed by a wall.
Comparative measures	Very simple tables of a few British/American/metric rounded-out equivalents, showing – if nothing else – the complications involved. See also **Proof**.

Metric	British		American
litres	pints	fl oz	oz
0·20		7	6¾
·50		17½	17
1	1	15¼	33 4/5
	gallons		gallons
5	1·1		1

British	American	Metric
fl oz	fl oz	litres
20 (1 pint)	19	0·56
16½	16 (1 pint)	0·47

In professional tables equivalents are shown to at least three decimal places; one can imagine the complexity of translating, say, a given number of litres at 45 Gay Lussac into the equivalent in British proof gallons.

Congeners (congenerics)	By-products inherent in small quantities to the processes of fermenting, distilling and maturing. They may be unwanted acids, esters, aldehydes and traces of other than ethyl alcohol. They may also be the essential constituents to the character of, say, whisky or brandy. Undesirable congeners disappear during maturation, or may be removed from spirit by rectification (redistillation) to purify the spirit before, or coincident with, flavouring; e.g. in producing quality gin.
Côte	Side of a hill, particularly found in Burgundy descriptions.
Crackling	American (English) translation of the French *pétillant;* slightly sparkling. The German is *spritzig*.
Cru	Literally 'growth'. See Bordeaux (Chapter 2). Another word often misleadingly used, as when *'grand cru'* is attached to important wine.
Cuvée	Wine drawn from a single vat; but is not infrequently mis-employed to indicate a vinous superiority a wine does not have.
Daisy	Old-fashioned name for a drink of spirit, fruit and syrup.
De luxe	Meaningless word unless attached to a totally reputable brand. Often misused, not being defined in law. See **Liqueur.**

Digestif	French description for any sweet liqueur or flavoured cordial; the other end of the scale from the aperitif, though those also are often sweet.
Domaine	'Estate'; the Burgundian equivalent to a Bordeaux *château.*
Dop	The South African equivalent of *Marc;* rough brandy.
Doux	'Soft' (French); descriptive of wines of sickly sweetness, normally without quality to redeem them.
Draff	Residue of mashing process in making beer or whisky; important cattle feed.
Dry	In spirits, means without added sugar. In wine may mean unsweetened, but in sherry often applies to what are in effect medium-dry. See **Sec, Brut.**
Eau de vie	'Water of life' – Generic term for spirit in France (from *aqua vitae*). Colloquially indicative of poor strong spirit, flavoured or plain, much of it rot-gut.
Feints	Unsatisfactory spirit produced in distillation (particularly in reference to whisky) which does not go into the finished product but is set aside for redistilling. The same applies to a lesser degree in the rectification of good gin; poor gin may contain the feints and they can make their unwelcome presence apparent.
Fiasco	Italian for flask.
Fluid ounce	One ounce of pure water (Britain). The American fluid ounce is one-sixteenth of a US pint; it is marginally larger than the British fl oz 20 oz = 1 pint.
Frappé	A drink served with finely crushed ice. See **Glacé.**
Fruit	Citrus fruits, when the rind is being used in mixed drinks, should be washed in warm water to remove preservative.
Fusel oil	General term for some unwanted congeners (qv).
Gallon	There are 1·2 US gallons for each British (imperial) gallon. There are six British standard bottles of spirit (26·6 fl oz) to a British gallon; five to a US gallon. A 'proof gallon' is one gallon of proof spirit. A 'wine' or 'bulk' gallon is a gallon of wine or spirit without regard to strength. See also **Metrication.**

Gauger One who gauges spirit: hence, in Scotland, a Customs officer.

Gill Quarter of a pint. British legal measures for public sale by the tot are described as '6-out' (of a gill); '5-out' (fifth of a gill or 1 fl oz); and '4-out' used in Ireland and sometimes called a 'club measure'.

Glacé A drink chilled by refrigeration or immersion in ice; not with ice in it. See **Frappé**.

Goût (French) 'taste'; as *'goût anglais'* sometimes used to describe very dry Champagne. Also means crude *eau de vie*.

Grog A tot of spirits, or a hot spirituous mix. Named for Admiral Vernon, the 18-century admiral whose nickname was Grogram and who started the practice of watering down before issue the very strong (discontinued) Royal Navy rum ration.

Grand vin Literally 'great wine'; whilst it often appears on the labels of fine vintages, as it has no real meaning it can also dignify indifferent ones; the phrase should be qualified by a reputed shipper to be meaningful.

Hydrometer The widely employed instrument invented by Christopher Sykes in early 19th century to bring science into the erstwhile crude methods of gauging the alcoholic strength of beverages. The proof system he devised and which is named after him provides great accuracy combined with extreme complexity. The hydrometer can, however, be adapted for the Gay Lussac system (see **Proof**). The adoption of this logical method is not part of Britain's programme of Metrication (qv) but a separate consideration. It is undecided as I write, but I am reliably informed that eventually the British proof system is doomed.

Jigger Another word for a measure.

Lees Dregs.

Litre See **Metrication.**

Liqueur Apart from its usual meaning, this misleading word is sometimes used colloquially to describe superior spirits, supposedly indicating they need no additive and are suitable for savouring post-prandially. It has no legal meaning.

Liquor In brewing and distilling terms, water. In American usage, spirits.

Measure For convenience I used this word in recipes. One can buy measures in various sizes; I recommend 1 oz.

Metrication Britain's decision to go metric in many particulars of daily life (an attitude not shared by the USA) with 1975 as the target date for a substantial completion of metrication, does not mean the automatic disappearance of traditional measures for British drinks. As matters stand, imperial units – gallons, pints, fluid ounces, etc. – must be used, and may be supplemented by metric. The current tendency is towards rounding out the metric content and giving this and the obligatory imperial equivalent on the label. There is no legal requirement regarding the quantities in which beer, cider or spirits are sold; they may be sold in any quantity, provided it be stated. This does not apply at present to imported wine. The effect will probably be that consumers will gradually get used to seeing metric quantities – if they read the labels at all – and will adjust to them rather as they have in the main adjusted to decimal coinage.

The EEC has been discussing standardising the quantities in which various wines, beers, liqueurs and spirits shall be sold, and have agreed on a few. However, these are only recommendations to member countries and their adoption is for individual decision. As a trading convenience, a majority may eventually opt for them. See **Hydrometer; Comparative Measures.**

Noble Rot *Pourriture noble';* the name in France for a fungus forming on grapes left to over-ripen for the making of fine sweet wines.

Phylloxera The scourge which, from the 1860s, devastated European, and other, vineyards. It was eventually defeated by grafting the European vines on to phylloxera-resistant American roots.

Plonk English slang for rough but sound wine; affectionately used as a rule. May derive from Cockney rhyming slang 'plink plonk' (vin blanc) of the first World War.

Potheen (Poteen)	Illicitly distilled Irish 'moonshine' whiskey; still a considerable bucolic industry.	
Premium	Another rather pointless phrase sometimes used colloquially to describe spirits of higher quality costing more than the standard prices.	
Prohibition	To settle arguments, it lasted in the USA from 1919 until nearly the the end of 1933.	
Proof	The metric Gay Lussac system is simplicity itself: 100 represents absolute alcohol and all strengths are given as percentages of that down to zero (water). The US Proof system is quite comprehensible when one realises that since absolute alcohol is 200 and that proof spirit 100, and is exactly 50/50 alcohol and water, it follows that if a spirit is marked, say, 90 proof US it contains 45 per cent alcohol. You simply halve the given US proof to obtain the alcohol content. Not so with British proof, with absolute alcohol (in practice) 175, and proof spirit represented by the figure 100, giving it no convenient alcohol strength but one of 57·14 per cent (to be pedantic). Some simple rounded-out comparisons:	

British proof	American proof	Gay Lussac (Percentage alcohol)
175	200	100
100*	114	57
88	100*	50
85	98	49
75	86	43
70	80	40
65	74	37

*(proof spirit)

It was once customary to use the terms over or under proof, and these are encountered in trade circles, but more usually the expression xx° or xx per cent proof are employed. If a spirit were over proof (OP) today it would most likely be marked, say, 115° proof. See also **Hydrometer.**

Punt	French for the indentation in the base of some wine bottles. It is a reinforcement in the instance of Champagne bottles. For some other wines it was originally for collecting the sediment. Also called *voleur* (thief). The English version is 'kick'.

Refilling	Supplanting the contents of a bottle with a similar product of lower quality than the original in order nefariously to obtain a higher profit.
Retsina	The resinated wine of Greece; an acquired taste, and rarely so acquired by non-Greeks.
Rickey	Type of drink said to be called after Joe Rickey, a well-known US Congressional lobbyist at the turn of the century. See Cocktails chapter.
Schiedam	Pioneer Dutch distilling centre. The town's name is sometimes used to describe Dutch gin. Now part of Rotterdam.
Schloss	German equivalent to château.
Sec	Literally 'dry' (French). In practice means sweetish. Demi-Sec means virtually the same, but possibly less sugary.
Silent (or neutral) spirit	Unflavoured grain or cane spirit.
Sommelier	A wine butler in a restaurant. Not just a waiter who serves wine; the term should only be applied to a man with some knowledge of his profession.
Sophisticated	In professional wine circles, a sophisticated wine is an adulterated one.
Specific gravity	The weight of a liquid (say, beer) as measured against the weight of a similar bulk of water.
Teetotal	Probably an American word, from 'total temperance' as opposed to simple temperance which formerly meant abstention from ardent spirits, not from beer or wine.
Trocken	'Dry' (German). When applied to grapes (*trockenbeeren*) it means the grapes have been dried on the stalk; they will be extremely rich in sugar. When applied to a wine, particularly a *sekt,* it indicates that the wine is dry.
Ullage	Spoiled beer. Also excessive air space in cask or bottle, causing deterioration of wine.

Recommended reading

I have, for this book, as for previous ones, not hesitated to call on certain authorities in confirmation of my own knowledge or, more often, to supplement it or refresh an over-burdened memory. In particular I would mention the totally invaluable *Encyclopaedia of Wines and Spirits* by Alexis Lichine (Cassell). This is not light reading, but it is a *sine qua non* for any serious drinker's shelf. Also essential, in my opinion are, *The Whiskies of Scotland* by Prof R J S McDowall (John Murray), the best short book about Scotch whisky, and *Wine* by Hugh Johnson (Sphere): Mr Johnson, all else apart, is the great defender of American wines. I owe a particular debt to these three authors.

There is a long list of books about Scotch whisky, those by Ross Wilson and David Daiches being notable amongst the more recent ones; both pretty erudite.

In paperbacks, Penguin's *Wines and spirits* by L W Morrison and *Book of Wine* by Allan Sichel are 'dippable' books but carry the stamp of expertise. The number of books about wine is enormous. Provided they are writing about an aspect that attracts you–and there are many aspects to wine– always have at least a look at books by Cyril Ray, Pamela Vandyke Price, E Penning-Rowsell, Harry Waugh (a great Claret man), and the late André Simon. On German wines no one knows more than Fritz Hallgarten, whose *Rhineland Wineland* is the definitive English language book on the subject. Written as a textbook for advanced hotel and catering industry students, Andrew Durkin's *Vendange–a study of wine and other drinks* (Arnold)– may be read with advantage by students in a much broader sense.

I have also found the following books important: *Dictionary of Drinks and Drinking*–by Oscar A Mendelsohn (Macmillan). *Grossman's Guide to Wines, and Spirits & Beers* by Harold J Grossman (Muller, London). *Wines & Spirits of the World*– ed Alec Gold (Virtue). I can only recommend as I know, and hope not to do injustice by omission.

But drinking is not just wine and spirits, nor simply their distillation. Books about *drinking,* about concocting drinks, can be fun as well as instructive. My favourite mixing book is David A Embury's *Fine Art of Mixing Drinks,* more anecdotal than the work of the many American authors of drink books; Faber were the British publishers. Many recipe books are admirable in themselves, but they lack the background information which makes other drink books entertaining to read. Entertaining indeed is Kingsley Amis' *On Drink* (Jonathan Cape); it is also concise, opinionated, instructive, and inexpensive, and has the bonus of Nicholas Bentley pictures. Mr Amis succeeds in what I tried to do in my Pan paperback *Booth's Handbook of Cocktails and Mixed Drinks.* (Modesty forbids my mentioning my other drinking tome but curious readers may find it mentioned at the beginning of this one.)

I would mention two excellent publications not available in normal commerce. One is *Off The Shelf* (second edition) by Anthony Hogg, which is published by Gilbey Vintners and, though it contains specific brand references, is extraordinarily well presented for a 'house' publication; although it is designed for the liquor trade, it has wider appeal. The other book is the United Kingdom Bartender's Guild's *International Guide to Drinks,* the official book of the International Bartender's Association. It can only be obtained through a member, or associate member, of the Guild, and is as useful a book as a dedicated amateur bartender could have, for its range is far-reaching.

This seems the moment when I should, for the third happy time, thank Mary Wallis for diligently sparing her own time from other multitudinous private activities to re-type my appalling originals, and for correcting my spelling, and (most of) my grammatical errors. And, far from least, I apologise to my wife for once again dislocating domestic life whilst preparing this work!

I know there are others to whom I should pay tribute or to whose works I should draw attention. All I will say is–and I know I am repeating myself– do not be too serious about drinking. Be it a Dry Martini or a milk shake, drinking is meant to be fun.

Index